A word from Sir Terry Wogan

As the saying goes, 'the way to a man's heart is through his stomach', so it's probably not much of a surprise that this book is a favourite of mine.

But, as many of you will know, my passion is for the BBC Children in Need Appeal for which I have been involved since the very first Appeal in 1980.

Rather like a great dish - the ingredients needed for the BBC Children in Need Appeal such as the money raised and the support given have, over the years, produced invaluable and extremely rewarding results in providing help to many thousands of disadvantaged children and young people in the UK. It amazes me more each year to see

so many people come together to help such a wonderful cause and I would like to thank all the chefs who have donated recipes and offered their support because, without them, this book would not be possible.

I would also like to thank Chris and his team at The Ransom Group, whose hard work and dedication have made this book possible for a second year running.

And to you, the reader, for your support in buying the book and thereby helping to raise money for the BBC Children in Need Appeal.

Now... where are my oven gloves?

Enjoy!

Terry Wogan

The BBC Children in Need Appeal

The BBC Children in Need appeal helps disadvantaged children and young people in the UK. Some have experienced domestic violence, neglect, homelessness or sexual abuse, while others have suffered from serious illnesses, or have had to learn to deal with profound disabilities from a very young age.

Many organisations supported by the charity aim to create a lasting impact on children's lives. Some offer low achieving children from areas of deprivation a chance to develop their educational skills and ambitions, and others create opportunities for young people who are homeless or socially excluded, to enable them to move forward and secure a fulfilling future.

The charity offers grants to voluntary and community groups and registered charities around the UK that focus on improving children's lives. Grants are targeted on the areas of greatest need, and money is allocated geographically to ensure that children in all corners of the UK have a fair share of the money raised.

For more information email: pudsey@bbc.co.uk or telephone: 020 8576 7788. You can also visit our website at: bbc.co.uk/pudsey.

In support of
BBC CHILDREN IN NEED

With thanks

Well, where do I start? There have been so many people involved in our second edition of 'This is my Favourite' that it would be impossible to mention everyone by name. My thanks go to all the 60 chefs without whom 'This is my Favourite' would not have been possible. I would however like to thank two in particular.

Firstly, Aldo Zilli, whose son Rocco was born this year making his involvement with the appeal and the book even more meaningful. Like Aldo, cooking has always been a passion within my family, with recipes being handed down from generation to generation and some of the tips I have learnt in the kitchen at the Zilli Cookery School this year are already being enjoyed by my family and friends. Thanks Aldo!

Secondly to Nick Vadis, British Airways Executive Chef, who in addition to donating a favourite recipe, is serving the 'My Favourite Night' dinner party menu (pages 100-105) to British Airways travellers during the week of the BBC Children in Need Appeal.

I would also like to thank Sir Terry Wogan whose kind words and support in writing the foreword to this year's book mean so much to all those involved. My thanks must also go, in no particular order, to the team at Ocado for making our suggested national dinner party menu ingredients available for everyone to order online. Also to Lara Rendell at thehut.com, our official online partner for ordering the book and to Susie Reid Thomas and her PR team at Silver Thread for helping raise awareness of the book.

And last but not least a big thanks to all my team at The Ransom Group - I couldn't have done it without you!

10 Contents

14
Dinner Party Menu
Adam Dickson

Appetizer: Wild Mushroom Pappardelle and Avocado

Main: English Fillet of Beef on Red Pepper and Aubergine Stack with Exmoor Blue Cheese Sauce

Dessert: Pressed Chocolate Cake

Appetizer

Main

Dessert

Adam Dickson

Born in New Zealand, Adam was raised and worked both there and in Queensland, Australia. He got his first break in cooking when he was just 15, although he tells us "there was hell to pay when they found out later that I was under-age!" He's developed his own style - what he calls 'modern eclectic fusion cuisine', which he says "blends the best of all worlds to tantalise the taste buds".

Appetizer: Wild Mushroom Pappardelle and Avocado

Chef Says

A perfect starter, thanks to the abundance of wild mushrooms in this country followed by ruby red Devon beef, and the dessert of the gods to finish; heaven on a plate!

Azure@livingcoasts
Harbourside
Beacon Quay
Torquay TQ1 2BG
Telephone: 01803 202499
www.livingcoasts.org.uk

In any good supermarket you will find all the ingredients but my advice is to get down to your local greengrocer or deli.

If picking your own wild mushrooms be very sure that you know what you are picking because many varieties are highly toxic or poisonous. Try looking on the internet for family day trips out with a qualified mycologist.

Keep your fungi friends in brown paper bags in the fridge, if they are in plastic bags they will go slimy.

If your avocado is like stone put it in your fruit bowl with your bananas for a few days or in a drawer or dark place. Don't forget it though, as rotten avocado isn't nice and you might end up with a tree in your drawer!

Serves: 1
Preparation time: 12-14 minutes

Ingredients:
70-100g wild mushrooms
150-200g pappardelle pasta
4 tablespoons olive oil
1/2 avocado de-stoned, fanned
1 clove garlic
100-150ml double cream
Salt and pepper to taste
1 sliced truffle (optional)
1 tablespoon or knob butter
Splash of white wine

For the garnish:
Balsamic vinegar reduction
Herb oil
Sun-dried tomato oil
Tortilla sail fried

Method:
1. In a saucepan cook off your pasta until al dente ('to the tooth') - don't over-cook it.
2. Bring water to the boil and add a tablespoon of olive oil, add the pasta and stir occasionally so it doesn't stick to the bottom of the pan.
3. Strain and run under cold water; this is called 'refreshing'.
4. In a frying pan add the olive oil and butter. Bring to a medium-to-high heat and add your mushrooms. Sauté off until nice and soft.
5. Add the garlic (try not to burn the garlic because the dish will become bitter) and a splash of white wine, reduce by 1/4 and then add the cream.
6. Reduce until reasonably thick and add the pasta. Toss through, thoroughly coating the pasta.
7. Add salt and pepper to taste.
8. On a nice serving plate arrange the pasta on the balsamic vinegar reduction, fan the avocado on top, garnish and serve. Hey presto! Wild mushroom pappardelle and avocado.

Main: English Fillet of Beef on Red Pepper and Aubergine Stack with Exmoor Blue Cheese Sauce

When buying fillet of beef check for a rich burgundy colour, this will be well hung/matured, the lighter the meat the shorter the hang or maturity. Shop locally and ask your butcher for your local shire cow.

This dish is so quick and easy it should only take you a few minutes. English beef is gorgeous!

Try adding wholegrain or English mustard, parmesan cheese, cheddar cheese or goat's cheese to the cream for a different sauce.

Ahh! Bisto! Gravy with a dash of red wine reduced by half; nice touch!

Serves: 1
Preparation time: 8-12 minutes
Cooking time:
blue - 4 minutes
rare - 6 minutes
medium rare - 8 minutes
medium - 10 minutes
medium well - 12 minutes

Ingredients:
285g fillet of beef
1 red pepper
4 rings aubergine
80-100g Exmoor blue cheese
100-150ml double cream
Salt and pepper to taste
100ml olive oil

Method:
1. Place the whole pepper on an oven proof tray and drizzle with olive oil. Place in a pre-heated oven on 180°C for around 10-15 minutes.
2. Remove and sweat in a bowl covered with cling film. Under cool running water peel off the skin then remove the seeds and slice into strips.
3. Now, in a bowl or mixing tub, place the aubergine rings and drizzle liberally with olive oil and season. Pan fry or chargrill the aubergine on both sides until soft then arrange aubergine and pepper on top of each other in a stack.
4. Pour the cream into a saucepan and crumble in the cheese. Using a whisk or wooden spoon keep it moving - don't let it stick or you will taste burnt cheese sauce.
5. Chargrill your beef to seal it. Place in the pre-heated oven - see cooking time.
6. Place fillet on stack and drizzle with sauce, garnish and serve. Nice, enjoy!

Dessert: Pressed Chocolate Cake

Try drizzling your favourite liqueur over the top or use pouring cream or a cracking ice cream. Clotted cream is a nice trick to tickle the taste buds.

Try serving with an assortment of seasonal fresh berries.

Remember chocolate is available all year round! And GO LOCAL for your berries or pick your own. Check out organic picking farms - cool!

The reason I make enough for 10 people is that whenever you make a cake or dessert you should always add a little for your friends and neighbours!

Serves: 10
Preparation time: 15-20 minutes
Cooking time: 30-40 minutes

Ingredients:

400g top quality bitter chocolate, broken into pieces
300g unsalted butter
10 eggs, separated (local organic free range where possible)
220g caster sugar
4 tablespoons of top quality cocoa powder

Method:

1. Pre-heat oven to 180°C. Grease a 27cm cake tin.
2. Melt the chocolate with the butter in a bowl over a pan of simmering water (the water should not touch the bottom of the bowl). Stir the chocolate until smooth. Remove the bowl from the top of the pan and allow it to cool.
3. Whisk the egg yolks and the sugar until nice and thick. Fold the egg yolk and sugar mix into the melted chocolate mix. Sieve the cocoa powder into the bowl and fold through.
4. Whisk the egg whites until soft peaks form then fold the egg whites into the chocolate mix, a quarter at a time.

5. Pour the mixture into the prepared cake tin and bake in the pre-heated oven for around 30–40 minutes, until the cake has risen like a soufflé and slightly set.
6. Remove from the oven when cooked and place a plate that fits inside the rim of the cake tin on top of the cake. Press down firmly on the plate allowing the edges to erupt around the rim of the plate. DO NOT PRESS TOO HARD! Place a light weight on top of the plate and allow to cool.

To Serve:

1. Remove cake from tin and portion. Warm portions through (suggest microwaving for 45-60 seconds, 1 portion approximately 25 seconds).
2. Serve with fresh strawberries and fresh Cornish clotted cream or a nice home-made ice cream. Gorgeous!

Ainsley Harriott

Ainsley's lifelong passion for cooking is a tribute to his mother, Peppy, who encouraged him to help cook for family and friends in what was always an open house in Balham, South London. Following the rules he learned from his mother, he advises people to "use fresh ingredients, have everything ready beforehand and never say it's too difficult!" His philosophy is that simple dishes can be just as good as fancy ones.

Monkfish on Crispy Potato Cakes

Chef Says

If you can't get pancetta use smoked streaky bacon and how about replacing one of the potatoes with the same amount of celeriac for a delicious nutty change?

Ainsley Harriott
TV Chef
Telephone: 020 7383 2000
www.jeremyhicks.com

Serves: **2**
Preparation time: **10 minutes**
Cooking time: **10 minutes**

Ingredients:
Monkfish
2 x 175g pieces of monkfish fillet, trimmed
4-6 long thin slices smoked pancetta
300ml chicken stock
85ml dry white wine
3 tablespoons double cream
25g butter
Leaves from 1 large sprig parsley, chopped
Salt and freshly ground black pepper

Crispy Potatoes
2 potatoes, 100-150g each, peeled
2 small shallots, peeled and finely chopped
1 egg, beaten
1 slightly rounded tablespoon self-raising flour
Sunflower oil for shallow frying

Method:
1. Wrap each piece of monkfish in 2-3 slices of pancetta, overlapping the edges slightly. Tie in a couple of places with some fine string and set aside.
2. Pre-heat the oven to 200ºC, 400ºF, Gas Mark 6. Put the stock, wine and cream into a small pan and boil until reduced to 85ml.
3. Heat half the butter in an ovenproof frying pan, add the monkfish, seam side up, and fry for 1-1½ minutes until golden brown. Turn over, transfer to the oven and roast for 10 minutes.

4. Meanwhile, finely grate the potatoes by hand or in a food processor. Working with small handfuls at a time, squeeze out as much excess liquid from them as you can. Put into a bowl, fork to separate into strands and mix in the shallots, egg, flour, a scant ½ teaspoon of salt and some pepper.
5. Heat 5mm sunflower oil in a clean frying pan, then reduce the heat to medium. Divide the potato mixture in half and shape into 4 thin circles 7.5cm wide. Fry in the oil for 3 minutes on each side until golden brown and crisp on the outside and cooked through in the centre. Drain briefly on kitchen paper and keep warm.
6. Remove the monkfish from the oven, turn the oven off, but leave the potato cakes inside. Transfer the fish to a plate and remove the string. Add the reduced chicken stock to the frying pan and bring to the boil, rubbing the base of the pan with a wooden spoon. Whisk in the remaining butter, stir in the parsley and season with a little salt and pepper.
7. Put the potato cakes in the centre of warmed plates and place the monkfish on top. Spoon around the sauce and serve with a green vegetable.

Taken from Ainsley's Friends and Family Cookbook.

Alan Coxon

Alan Coxon, the UK's leading food archaeologist and celebrity chef was born in Derbyshire before moving to France at the age of twelve. It was this exposure to French culinary influences that inspired Alan to become a chef. Alan is very much committed to the furthering of food understanding through its origins, including the influences of Roman, Egyptian and Ancient Greek cuisines, and was recently voted as one of the top 10 favourite TV chef presenters of the world by a poll carried out by BBC Food.

Javanese Style Chicken

Chef Says

To keep the salad looking crisp always return the washed leaves back to the fridge for 30 minutes before serving and never dress a salad until the last minute as acids within the dressing will start to cook the leaves.

www.alancoxon.com
Telephone: 020 8876 7566

Serves: 4
Preparation time: 15 minutes
Cooking time: 20 minutes

Ingredients:
Chicken
Allow 1 x 240g chicken breast per portion
2 teaspoons ground coriander
2 teaspoons ground cumin
2 teaspoons ground cloves
2 teaspoons ground turmeric
2 shallots, finely chopped
2 red chillies, finely diced
2 tablespoons lemon juice
4 tablespoons vegetable oil (2 for oiling the tray)
120g brown sugar
Salt and pepper

Fresh Crisp Salad
450g salad leaves - a selection of 4 varieties from the following: baby bok choi, baby spinach, escarole, oakleaf, lambs, baby gems. The leaves should be separated, washed and dried.
50g flat leaf parsley, washed and dried
50g picked chervil leaves
50g chives, snipped
If entertaining, add some of the following flowers to the salad; chive flowers, pansies, rosemary flowers, thyme flowers. All of these add flavour and turn a salad into a feast for the eyes.

Quick Spring Onion Relish
3 tablespoons sesame seeds
1 bunch (approx 8) spring onions, chopped
2 teaspoons fresh ginger, grated
1½ tablespoons light soy sauce
2 teaspoons rice wine vinegar or

2 teaspoons dry sherry
1 tablespoon sesame oil
1 teaspoon clear honey

Method:
Chicken
1. Pre-heat the oven to 200ºC, 400ºF, Gas Mark 6.
2. Make 4 small incisions across the breasts of the chicken with a small sharp knife.
3. Place all the chicken ingredients into a bowl and mix well. Massage into the breasts and incisions.
4. Place the chicken breasts onto a lightly oiled tray or roasting pan, rubbing in all the marinade.
5. Season with salt and pepper.
6. Place into the pre-heated oven and cook for approximately 18-20 minutes, or until cooked through.
7. When ready, serve with the fresh dressed salad, and quick spring onion relish for maximum flavour. Simple, light and very healthy.

Fresh Crisp Salad
1. Place the prepared ingredients into a bowl, keeping them light, fresh and clean.
2. Just before serving add the dressing to the salad leaves and gently toss to coat.
3. Serve the Javanese Style Chicken on the top with a little spring onion relish.

Quick Spring Onion Relish
1. Place all ingredients into a food processor and blend briefly until a coarse pulp has been achieved.
2. Place in a serving bowl and serve.

22
Vegetarian Dinner Party Menu
Aldo Zilli

Appetizer: Grilled Field Mushrooms with Dolcelatte

Main: Sun-dried Tomato, Goat's Cheese and Rocket Risotto

Dessert: Panna Cotta with Fruits of the Forest

Appetizer

Main

Dessert

Aldo Zilli

Aldo Zilli is the founder and chef patron of one of London's most exciting restaurant groups which incorporates Zilli Café, Zilli Fish and Signor Zilli Restaurant & Bar. He has also featured on 'Celebrity Fit Club' for ITV1, starred in 'The Weakest Link Chef Special' and 'Wish You Were Here' from his home region of Abruzzo. Aldo makes regular appearances on 'Good Food Live' on the UK Food Channel. Aldo's latest TV appearance was as one of four of 'The Chefs' quartet on 'Celebrity X Factor, Battle of the Stars', where he wowed the audience and the judges with his vocal skills... and dance moves!

Appetizer: Grilled Field Mushrooms with Dolcelatte

Chef Says

Great, simple dish as a starter. Ideally use the small portobellini field mushrooms serving three per person. If using the large portobello field mushroom, you will only need 4 large mushrooms, allowing one per person.

Zilli Fish
36-40 Brewer Street
London W1F 9TA
Telephone: 020 7734 8649
www.zillialdo.com

To serve as a party nibble, only use the portobellini, placing each mushroom on small crostini to make them into tidy finger food.

To make crostini, slice small rounds from a ciabatta, brush with olive oil on both sides and bake until golden brown and crisp on both sides. Allow to cool before using.

Dolcelatte is a rich, creamy soft blue cheese from Italy. If you prefer, it can be substituted with Gorgonzola.

Serves: 4
Preparation time: 15 minutes
Cooking time: 10 minutes

Ingredients:
12 small-medium field mushrooms
2 tablespoons extra virgin olive oil
1 garlic clove, finely chopped (optional)
Juice of 1 lemon
1 tablespoon fresh breadcrumbs
1 teaspoon ground black pepper
100g soft Dolcelatte
2 tablespoons double cream
40g parmesan cheese, freshly grated
2 tablespoons flat leaf parsley, freshly chopped

Method:
1. Brush the mushrooms clean and remove the stalks. Finely chop the stalks and reserve. Place the mushrooms on a grill tray, stalk-side up.
2. In a glass bowl mix the olive oil, garlic, lemon, breadcrumbs and pepper. Stir in the finely chopped stalks. Spoon into the centre of each mushroom and grill for 5 minutes.
3. Meanwhile, place the cheese and cream in a small pan and melt over a gentle heat, stirring to combine.
4. Spoon the Dolcelatte mixture over the mushrooms, sprinkle with parmesan and grill for a further 5 minutes or until golden. Serve with a sprinkle of Italian parsley.

Main: Sun-dried Tomato, Goat's Cheese and Rocket Risotto

This risotto has a clean white finish from the goat's cheese melting into the rice which is then speckled with the strong red sun-dried tomatoes and bright green rocket. If possible it tastes even better than it looks!

A good goat's cheese to use is soft caprino, but as an alternative use the one that comes in small thick rounds with an edible rind - this is the type that can be easily sliced for grilling without losing its shape. This cheese can also be stored in a large jar of flavoured extra virgin olive oil with herbs. The soft, light-textured goat's cheeses are not suitable for this dish.

Serves: 4
Preparation time: 20 minutes
Cooking time: 30 minutes

Ingredients:
100g butter
1 large onion, chopped
1 bay leaf
350g arborio or carnaroli risotto rice
200ml dry white wine such as verdicchio
1 litre vegetable stock
100g sun-dried tomatoes in oil, drained and sliced
100g goat's cheese, diced
25g parmesan cheese, freshly grated
4 thin slices of goat's cheese
50g rocket, washed and cut into pieces

Method:
1. Take a large deep frying pan and melt 75g butter, add the onion and bay leaf and cook for 5 minutes until the onion is soft.
2. Stir the rice into the onion mixture until all the grains are glistening with butter, cook for 1 minute. Mix in the white wine and cook for 2 minutes until the wine has evaporated. Meanwhile pour the stock into a separate saucepan and heat gently. Add a ladleful of hot stock to the rice, stir and cook for 3-4 minutes until the liquid is absorbed. Continue in this way until all or nearly all the stock has been absorbed or until the rice is 'al dente'. This process should take about 18-20 minutes.
3. 15 minutes into the cooking of the risotto, stir in the cubed goat's cheese, sun-dried tomatoes and rocket. Cook for 3 minutes, adding stock as needed. The cheese should not melt completely.
4. Add the remaining butter and parmesan to the risotto and season to taste with salt and freshly ground black pepper. Cover and leave to rest for 1 minute. Meanwhile, put the slices of goat's cheese on a foil-lined grill pan and grill under a pre-heated grill for 1-2 minutes until golden. Serve the risotto with a slice of grilled goat's cheese on top finished with a twist of black pepper.

Dessert: Panna Cotta with Fruits of the Forest

This is a cooked cream dessert which is very simple yet luxurious. It keeps for up to 3-4 days in the fridge. It's best made with a vanilla pod as the seeds that fall into the cream mixture give it that characteristic fresh vanilla flavour and appearance.

When using fresh vanilla pods, do not throw them away after use, simply place in a pot of sugar. 1-2 days later you will have vanilla sugar, perfect for sprinkling over fresh fruit.

Serves: 4
Preparation time: 20 minutes
Cooking time: 10 minutes
(3 hours chilling)

Ingredients:

Panna Cotta
3-4 tablespoons caster sugar
300ml double cream
300ml milk
1 vanilla pod, halved lengthways
175g mascarpone cheese
2 level teaspoons gelatin granules
2 tablespoons Marsala
Sunflower oil for brushing

Fruits of the Forest Compote
100g caster sugar
50ml water
Finely grated rind of 1 lime
Juice from $^{1}/_{2}$ a lime
2 sprigs fresh mint
50g each blackberries, blueberries and strawberries, slicing or halving the blackberries and strawberries if large

Method:

1. Simmer the sugar, cream, milk and vanilla pod for 5-8 minutes stirring occasionally. Remove vanilla pod, wash clean and store to use again.

2. Remove pan from the heat and whisk the mascarpone into the hot cream. Put the Marsala in a bowl and stir in gelatin granules, leave it to swell, then stand over boiling water until the gelatin has dissolved. Mix into the warm cream.

3. Lightly oil four 200ml ramekins or glass pots and pour in the cream. Chill for 3 hours or overnight until set. To turn out the panna cotta, dip each ramekin in a bowl of hot water for 30 seconds and invert onto serving plates or bowls, give them a good shake to release.

4. About 30 minutes before serving make the fruit compote. Dissolve the sugar in the water then boil for 1 minute. Allow the syrup to cool for 5 minutes before adding the lime zest, juice, mint and fruits. Leave to cool.

5. Discard the mint sprigs then spoon the fruits and syrup around the panna cotta to serve.

Alfred Prasad

Alfred moved to London in June 1999 and worked as Sous Chef at Veeraswamy before joining Tamarind. Today, Alfred has gained industry and public recognition for his cuisine - he was named in the Restaurant Magazine's top twenty 'movers and shakers' for 2004, as well as one of the 'rising stars' predicted to make it big in 2004 in Delicious Magazine. Alfred was also added to the 2004 Debrett's People of Today, the annual publication which showcases great achievers in British society.

Grilled Salmon with Lime-leaf and Coriander

Chef Says

The delicate flavour of grilled salmon with the freshness of lime-leaf, mint and coriander - excellent on its own or as part of a delicious salad.

Tamarind
20 Queen Street
London W1J 5PR
Telephone: 020 7629 3561
www.tamarindrestaurant.com

Serves: **2**
Preparation time: **30 minutes**
Cooking time: **10 minutes**

Ingredients:
Salmon
500g salmon fillet
½ a lemon
1 tablespoon ginger-garlic paste
½ teaspoon salt

Paste
80g spinach
80g coriander leaves
60g mint leaves
15g lime-leaf
6 small green chillies
1 tablespoon lemon juice
2 tablespoons vegetable oil
1 tablespoon gram flour
2 tablespoons yoghurt
Salt to taste

Method:
1. De-scale the salmon fillet, leaving the skin on, wash well and cut it into cubes roughly 2 inches square.
2. Sprinkle the juice of ½ a lemon over the cubes of salmon, add a tablespoon of ginger-garlic paste and ½ a teaspoon of salt, mix together and leave aside.
3. For the paste, chop the lime-leaves and coriander leaves roughly, pick the leaves of mint off the stalks and wash all the leaves together in cold standing water. Lift the leaves out of the standing water and place in a strainer.
4. Put the drained leaves into a food processor along with green chillies, a tablespoon of lemon juice and 2 tablespoons of vegetable oil. Blend into a paste.
5. Transfer paste to a bowl and add 1 tablespoon of gram flour, 2 tablespoons of yoghurt and salt to taste. Whisk together and apply over cubes of salmon.
6. Marinate for 20 minutes.
7. Cook in a medium hot oven for 10 minutes and under a grill for a couple of minutes.

28
Andrew Pern

Self taught to a degree, Andrew's northern roots inspire and are apparent in his cooking. He takes traditional British style, anglicised classics and adds a twist with his use of regional, seasonal produce from both local amateur and national professional suppliers and producers. Constantly on the look-out for new ingredients, his use of all things local has, over the years, become his trademark.

Roast Loin of Suffolk Lamb with Asparagus, Creamed Goat's Cheese and Lavender Vinaigrette

Chef Says

This dish is 'Provence meets Yorkshire'; French flavours combined with the best Yorkshire ingredients. Lowna goat's cheese from the Yorkshire Wolds, local asparagus from the Vale of York, local lamb and lavender. "This" says Andrew, "is summer on a plate!"

Top tip - Use the freshest and most local produce available and early in season asparagus is the best.

The Star Inn
High Street
Harome
York
North Yorkshire YO62 5JE
Telephone: 01439 770397
www.thestaratharome.co.uk

Serves: 4
Preparation time: **15 minutes**
Cooking time: **15 minutes**

Ingredients:
4 x 115g lamb loins from the saddle
2 teaspoons Pommery mustard
2 sprigs lavender leaves, roughly chopped
2 Grosmont goat's cheese or any soft variety of goat's cheese each weighing approx 100g
1 teaspoon whipping cream
1 teaspoon black peppercorns, cracked
1 teaspoon chives, finely chopped
Olive oil for frying
200g wild rocket leaves and soft garden herbs such as oregano or flat-leaf parsley
12 medium asparagus spears

Garlic Croutons
2 slices wholemeal bread
115g butter, softened
1 clove garlic, crushed

Vinaigrette
3 tablespoons each of Pommery mustard, extra virgin olive oil and cider vinegar
1 teaspoon runny honey

Method:
1. Trim the lamb loins, roll them in the grain mustard and then the chopped lavender leaves. Wrap tightly in cling film and chill until ready to cook.
2. For the garlic croutons, pre-heat the oven to 190°C, 375°F. Remove the crusts from the bread and cut into 1cm cubes. Melt the butter in a small pan with the garlic - do not let it boil. Add the bread cubes and stir until thoroughly coated with butter. Place on a small baking sheet and bake in the pre-heated oven for 8 minutes until crisp and golden. Leave to cool.
3. For the mustard and honey vinaigrette, simply whisk all the ingredients together.
4. Cream the goat's cheese in a blender for 2-3 minutes adding a touch of cream to slacken if necessary, the mixture should stand in peaks. Season with cracked black peppercorns and chives.
5. Unwrap the lamb. Heat a little oil in a frying pan and fry the meat for 2-3 minutes on each side until an even crust forms. Lift out of the pan and rest.
6. Pipe or spoon 3 pyramids of goat's cheese at triangular points on 4 plates. Arrange the wild rocket garden herbs and croutons in the centre of the plate and 1 asparagus spear between each pyramid. Cut each lamb loin into 5 slices and arrange on top of the salad.
7. Drizzle some vinaigrette around the plate and over the lamb to give it a little shine and serve immediately.

30
Antony Worrall Thompson

Antony Worrall Thompson is a restaurateur and one of the most familiar and popular TV chefs. He presents 'Saturday Cooks' and is a regular guest chef on 'This Morning'. He is increasingly in demand by broadcasters to comment on and discuss serious food issues such as diabetes, obesity, nutrition and the eating habits of children. He has his own smallholding and breeds Middle White pigs for the pork which he serves in his restaurants.

Rhubarb and Ginger Eton Mess

Chef Says

Rhubarb and ginger make a good springtime alternative to the traditional strawberry version.

www.awtonline.co.uk

Serves: 4
Preparation time: 10 minutes

Ingredients:
560g can rhubarb, drained
(or roast your own)
1 tablespoon stem ginger in syrup, chopped
425ml whipping cream
3 tablespoons caster sugar
100g meringues, broken up into bite size pieces (shop bought is fine)

Method:
1. Mix together the rhubarb and ginger.
2. Whip the cream and sugar together until soft peaks form.
3. Spoon some cream into the bottom of a bowl, scatter over some meringue and fruit mixture followed by more cream and repeat until full.

Barny Haughton

Quartier Vert (QV), the restaurant, was born out of a desire to return to European traditions; simple cooking using local, organic ingredients. The business has since grown to include a cookery school, a bakery and catering. Barny's philosophy is simple; good food depends on good cooking; good cooking depends on good produce; good produce depends on good agricultural practices. Barny and the QV team put real food and real values back on the menu of everyday life!

Saltimbocca Alla Romana with Soft Polenta and Roast Winter Vegetables

Chef Says

These are little sandwiches of veal or pork filled with prosciutto, sage and lemon zest. Saltimbocca is Italian for 'jump in the mouth'. Why veal? Veal is to beef what lamb is to mutton. Without veal calves there is no butter, milk, yoghurt, cheese or a hundred other food products we take for granted. You should buy pink (ideally organic) veal. Talk to a good butcher!

Top tip - use seasonal vegetables to accompany the dish. Try purple sprouting broccoli in the spring, broad beans and peas in the summer and slow roast tomatoes and garlic in the autumn.

Quartier Vert
85 Whiteladies Road
Clifton
Bristol BS8 2NT
Telephone: 0117 973 4482
www.quartiervert.co.uk

Serves: 4
Preparation time: 40 minutes
Cooking time: 45-50 minutes

Ingredients:

Saltimbocca
600g of topside veal or trimmed pork loin
4 slices prosciutto
4-6 fresh sage leaves, roughly chopped
Zest of 1 lemon
Salt and pepper

Polenta
100g ground polenta
400ml water or half water and milk
Knob of butter
1 handful of parmesan, freshly grated

Roasted Winter Vegetables
2 red onions, peeled
2 carrots, peeled
1/2 butternut squash, peeled and deseeded
1/2 swede, peeled
8 whole, unpeeled garlic cloves
Fresh thyme
3 tablespoons olive oil
Salt and pepper

Method:

1. Pre-heat the oven to 220ºC, 425ºF, Gas Mark 7.
2. Cut the veal into 8 equal slices and bash gently with a rolling pin to flatten until they are thin, like rashers of bacon. Place a slice of prosciutto, the chopped sage, lemon zest and a little seasoning on 4 of the pieces of veal. Put the other pieces on top to create 4 neat sandwiches and refrigerate.
3. Cut the vegetables into large chunks (1-1½ inches) and place in a roasting tray, add the garlic cloves and a few sprigs of thyme. Drizzle over the olive oil, season with salt and pepper, toss well and place in a pre-heated oven for 40-45 minutes.
4. Meanwhile, make some soft polenta by stirring 100g of ground polenta into 400ml of gently boiling salted water until a thick, porridge consistency is achieved. Keep stirring occasionally for 30 minutes or so over a very gentle heat. You may need to add some more liquid. When you are ready to eat, add a generous knob of butter and a handful of freshly grated parmesan and stir well. It should be soft and creamy in consistency and yellow in colour.
5. Frying the saltimbocca takes 50 seconds. Heat a little butter and olive oil in a frying pan. When almost smoking hot, put in the saltimbocca; 25 seconds on one side and then 25 seconds on the other.
6. Serve immediately with the polenta and the roasted vegetables.

Saltimbocca Alla Romana with Soft Polenta and Roast Winter Vegetables **Barny Haughton** ■

Photography by Nick Hand

Bernhard Mayer

Bernhard joined Four Seasons Hotels & Resorts at the Regent Hong Kong as Executive Chef in 1999 and transferred to the Regent Jakarta in July 2001. On returning to London, Bernhard says: "After spending time in the Far East, I enjoy pairing fresh British produce with Asian flavours to create new dishes for the menu in our Lanes Restaurant. Our guests are well-travelled and discerning so it is an exciting challenge to keep up with their changing tastes and requirements."

Sautéed Lobster with Wasabi-cucumber Risotto and Pink Ginger

Chef Says

This is a real favourite as it combines good strong flavours of the East and fabulous colours make it so pleasing to the eye.

Top tip - when finishing the risotto make sure the rice has a runny consistency for a lighter taste.

Four Seasons Hotel
Hamilton Place
Park Lane
London W1A 1AZ
Telephone: 020 7499 0888
www.fourseasons.com/london

Serves: **6**
Preparation time: **30 minutes**
Cooking time: **45 minutes**

Ingredients:
240g carnaroli rice
200ml white wine
20g shallots, chopped
1 garlic clove, crushed
300ml fish stock
300ml cucumber juice
50ml whipped cream
100g parmesan cheese, grated
30g wasabi paste
1 cucumber, without seeds, diced
60ml sushi vinegar
6 small lobsters
1 red chilli
Pink ginger

Method:
Preparation
1. Blanch the lobsters in boiling water for 6 minutes and then cool in iced water.
2. When cold, break the flesh out of the shell including the claw meat (but extract the bone inside) and the tail meat. Cut the tail meat into 2cm chunks. Keep to one side until ready to serve.

Risotto
1. Pour a film of olive oil in a sauté pan and heat gently, add the rice and cook until translucent.
2. Add the shallots and garlic just so they heat.
3. Add the white wine and reduce until dry then slowly start to incorporate the fish stock and cucumber juice. Slowly cook the rice until almost all the liquid is absorbed.
4. When the rice is soft but still has some bite to it add the wasabi paste and parmesan cheese.
5. To finish, season with the sushi vinegar, salt and pepper.
6. Keep hot on the side while cooking the lobster.

Lobster
1. To cook the lobster, heat a film of oil in a pan, season the lobster with salt and pepper and then sauté until cooked. The meat will turn a little white but will still be opaque in colour.
2. When the lobster is cooked, add the diced cucumber and serve on top of the risotto. Garnish with chilli slices and pink ginger.

Brian Turner CBE

Brian Turner is one of Britain's most successful and well-known chefs. In addition to running highly respected restaurants in the UK, he has become a successful television personality, still appearing regularly on 'Ready Steady Cook' and 'Great Food Live'.

Roast Fillet of Beef with Foie Gras, Fondant Potatoes Stuffed with Garlic Mushrooms and Coriander Carrots

Chef Says

Old fashioned and classical this dish may be, but the flavours and the marriage of the ingredients are fantastic.

Brian Turner Mayfair
Millennium Hotel,
London Mayfair
Grosvenor Square
London W1K 2HP
Telephone: 020 7596 3444
www.brianturner.co.uk

Serves: 4
Preparation time: 40 minutes
Cooking time: 1¼ hours

Ingredients:
Beef
700g piece fillet of beef
1 head of garlic
1 tablespoon oil
25g butter
Salt and pepper
4 slices foie gras
2 shallots, chopped
½ glass dry Madeira

1 glass dry white wine
¼ pint meat stock
Corn flour to thicken
1 tablespoon parsley, chopped

Fondant Potatoes
2 large potatoes
1 tablespoon oil
25g butter
½ pint chicken stock
Salt and pepper
110g button mushrooms
1 clove garlic
25g butter
1 tablespoon parsley, chopped

Coriander Carrots
450g carrots
50g butter
2 tablespoons coriander, chopped
Salt and pepper
2 tablespoons double cream

Method:
Beef
1. Trim the beef of nerve. Tie with string to retain the shape, rub well with garlic and cut in half.
2. Heat the oil in a roasting tray. Add the butter, put the beef in and seal all round. Put into the oven at 210°C. Roast for approximately 20 minutes, then take out and leave to rest.
3. In the roasting tray, lightly colour the shallots. Add the Madeira and white wine.
4. Trim the foie gras to shape and chop up the trimmings. Add the trimmings to the roasting tray. Add the stock and cook together. Cook for 5 minutes and strain into a clean pan. Season and thicken slightly with corn flour.

5. Heat a dry frying pan. Sear the foie gras pieces and put to one side.
6. Remove the string from the beef and cut into 4 even steaks. Put onto a plate with potatoes and carrots, cut side up. Put the foie gras on top of the meat. Serve the sauce around and apart.

Fondant Potatoes
1. Cut the peeled potatoes into 4 slices across the potato, 1 inch thick. Using a cutter, cut the potatoes into a round shape. Using a Parisian spoon, take a half ball from the middle of the potato.
2. Heat the oil in a roasting tray. Add the butter. Put the potatoes in with the cut side down and colour until golden brown.
3. Turn over, season and put in the stock to reach half way up the potato. Cook in the oven until golden brown, cooked and the stock evaporated. Top up if necessary.
4. Meanwhile cut the mushrooms into small dice. Sauté in butter with crushed garlic. Season and add parsley.
5. When the potatoes are ready, fill the hole with the mushrooms and serve one per person.

Coriander Carrots
1. Peel, top and tail the carrots. Cut in half lengthwise and cut in rough triangle shapes. Melt the butter, add the carrots and season.
2. Stew slowly for about 30 minutes until soft. Do not colour. Add a little water if needed. When cooked add the cream and boil until thickened.
3. Check seasoning, add the coriander and season.

Roast Fillet of Beef with Foie Gras, Fondant Potatoes and Coriander Carrots **Brian Turner CBE** ■

Chris Wicks

Bell's Diner is without doubt one of Bristol's more serious food establishments. Opened in 1976 the restaurant is now run by chef-proprietor Christopher Wicks. Chris and his young team of chefs cook modern, contemporary British food with a firm Mediterranean influence.

Coconut Mousse, Lime Salt, Vindaloo Ice Cream and Poppadom Tuile

Chef Says

Don't be put off by the curry flavoured ice cream, it really works well with the whole recipe.

Top tip - lightly whip the cream so that it barely holds a peak and allow the gelatine and coconut mix to set to the consistency of the whipped cream before folding together.

Bell's Diner
1 York Road
Montpelier
Bristol B56 5QB
Telephone: 0117 924 0357
www.bellsdiner.co.uk

Ingredients:

Nut Base
85g peanuts
40g dark chocolate
40g crackle crystals
2 teaspoons ground cardamom

Coconut Anglaise
400ml double cream
600ml coconut milk
200g egg yolks
100g unrefined caster sugar

Mousse
600ml coconut anglaise
400ml whipping cream
10g bronze leaf gelatine

Vindaloo Ice Cream
630ml whole milk
50g milk powder
120g unrefined caster sugar
6 medium egg yolks
2 tablespoons vindaloo curry paste

Lime Salt
3 limes

Chocolate Box
300g dark chocolate
Plastic acetate

Method:

Nut Base

1. Roast the nuts in the oven until golden and grind into a powder.
2. Melt the chocolate in a double boiler, stir in the nut powder, crackle crystals and cardamom. Press into individual ring moulds 5mm deep.

Coconut Anglaise

1. Boil the coconut milk, cream and 40g of sugar. Whisk the rest of the sugar with the egg yolks until light and fluffy.
2. Pour the milk and cream onto the egg mixture, whisking vigorously. Cover with cling film and allow to cool. Strain into a bowl.

Mousse

1. Soak the gelatine in cold water until softened, squeeze out excess water and stir into warm anglaise and chill.
2. Lightly whip the cream and fold into the anglaise when it has set to the consistency of double cream. Fill up ring moulds and chill.

Vindaloo Ice Cream

1. Boil the milk, milk powder and half the sugar. Whisk the rest of the sugar with the egg yolks. Pour the milk onto the egg mixture, whisking vigorously. Strain and allow to cool, cover with cling film.
2. Stir in the curry paste then churn in ice cream machine.

Lime Salt

1. Finely grate the limes and dry on a silicone sheet in a warm oven.

Chocolate Box

1. Cut plastic to fit the height and circumference of the moulds. Coat with chocolate and allow to dry.
2. Coat a large sheet with chocolate then place another one on top. Weight down to prevent bending and chill.

To Serve:

1. Snap poppadoms into quarters, deep fry and dust with cocoa powder.
2. Warm ring mould with hot cloth or blow torch and slip off. Cover sides with the chocolate acetate neatly (plastic on outside) and chill. Peel the large plastic sheet and cut chocolate lids with a ring mould. Place the mousse onto a plate, peel off the plastic and carefully top with a lid. Serve with a scoop of ice cream and poppadom. Sprinkle with lime salt.

Darren Comish

Darren Comish, like the founder of Miller Howe John Tovey MBE, was born in Barrow-in-Furness on the edge of the glorious Lake District. They share a passion for local produce, meats and fish cooked to perfection.

Goat's Cheese Cheesecake

Chef Says

I chose this dish because it is light and refreshing and is one of our restaurant's top sellers.

Darren Comish
Miller Howe Hotel
Rayrigg Road
Windermere LA23 1EY
Telephone: 01539 442536
www.millerhowe.com

Serves: **10**
Preparation time: **45 minutes**

Ingredients:
Goat's Cheese
1 x goat's cheese log
500g mascarpone cheese
Juice of 1 lemon

Celery Jelly
1 head celery
Pinch of salt
Pinch of sugar
7 leaves gelatine (soaked)

Apple Sorbet
Skins of 6 Granny Smith apples, frozen
750g sugar
650ml water
60g glucose

Apple Purée
3 Granny Smith apples
30g caster sugar
Knob of butter

Hazelnut Crumble
Handful of hazelnuts, chopped and peeled
500g flour
300g butter
250g sugar

Method:
Goat's Cheese Cheesecake
1. Peel the rind off the goat's cheese then heat until soft, adding mascarpone and lemon juice. Leave at room temperature.

Celery Jelly
1. Juice the head of celery and season with salt and sugar. Warm gently and add gelatine. Pass through a muslin cloth and refrigerate.

Apple Sorbet
1. Put sugar, water and glucose in a pan and boil until it becomes a syrup. Allow it to cool.
2. Add the frozen apple skins and purée in a blender. Then pass through a chinois.
3. Churn in an ice-cream machine and freeze for at least 4 hours.

Apple Purée
1. Add all ingredients to a pan and heat gently and slowly until the apples become soft. Purée in a blender and pass through a chinois.

Hazelnut Crumble
1. Crumble flour, butter and sugar together, then add the chopped hazelnuts.
2. Blitz both ingredients together and bake until golden. Blitz again in the blender and set aside.

To Assemble:
1. Form a round of goat's cheese cheesecake by scooping it up between two spoons and place on one side of the plate.
2. Cover with crumble. Spread a line of purée along the plate, add a disc of jelly and place some sorbet on the top.

42
Dipak Modak

Now nationally renowned for its vegetarian fare, Bobby's first opened in 1976 and was the first Indian vegetarian restaurant of its kind. Still run by the same family, it maintains its strong principles around vegetarianism and the use of fresh ingredients.

Bhindi Masala

Chef Says

This recipe removes those common myths that imply that Indian dishes are too spicy or heavy for everyday consumption, by focusing on keeping the natural flavours and goodness of the fresh ingredients.

Top tip - don't be tempted to add water, the steam generated from the ingredients will do the trick!

Bobby's Restaurant
154/6 Belgrave Rd
Leicester LE4 5AT
Telephone: 0116 2660106
www.eatatbobbys.com

Serves: 2
Preparation time: 15 minutes
Cooking time: 22 minutes

Ingredients:

4 tablespoons sunflower oil
200g onion, finely chopped
(approx 2 small onions)
2 teaspoons freshly ground ginger
2 teaspoons freshly ground garlic
½ teaspoon turmeric powder
1 teaspoon coriander powder
1 teaspoon chilli powder
2 teaspoons cumin (jeera) powder
1 teaspoon salt
½ teaspoon garam masala
2 medium red tomatoes
400g okra (approx 50 fingers)
Fresh coriander and slices of lemon
for garnish

Method:

1. Finely chop the onions, tomatoes and coriander.
2. Remove top and tail of the okra and centre slice to three quarters of the length.
3. Grind the garlic and ginger into a paste.
4. Heat the oil in a heavy non-stick wok, add the onions and cook on medium heat for approximately 5 minutes until lightly gold.
5. Add the garlic and ginger paste, stir and mix well before adding the chopped tomatoes.
6. Turn the heat to simmer and add the salt, coriander powder, turmeric powder, cumin powder and chilli powder. Stir gently for 2 minutes.
7. Raise to a medium heat, add the okra and stir well. Cover and allow to cook for 10 minutes, stirring at 5 minute intervals.
8. Add the garam masala, stir in well and cook for a final 5 minutes. Garnish with coriander and lemon slices.
9. Serve in a decorative wok with a hot chapati or naan bread.

Drogo Montagu

Drogo has worked all over the world, most notably in the Hotel Walserhof in Switzerland which has 2 Michelin stars. He is now Head Chef at the exclusive Mamilanji Club in London's Kings Road where his recent guests have included the Take That entourage and the Bolivian Ambassador.

Seared Tuna Teriyaki

Chef Says

Although this dish can be served all year round, it is most suited to the summer months due to its delicate clean taste. The simplicity and combination of flavours will make this a dish you will want to use many times.

Mamilanji Club
107 Kings Road
London SW3 4PA
Telephone: 020 7351 5521
www.mamilanji.com

Serves: 6
Preparation time: 20 minutes
Cooking time: 5 minutes

Ingredients:
Teriyaki Sauce
150ml plum sauce
100g oyster sauce
25ml sesame oil
10 drops fish sauce
5ml mirin
Zest of 2 limes
Juice of 1 lime
1/2 tablespoon ginger, grated
1/2 teaspoon garlic, grated
1 tablespoon chilli, finely diced
15g coriander leaves, finely chopped

Tuna
1kg fresh tuna (sashimi grade if possible)
2 tablespoons olive oil for frying
2 limes for garnish

Method:
1. Put a non-stick frying pan over a high heat with olive oil.
2. Season the tuna generously with sea salt and pepper.
3. Sear each side of tuna for 30 seconds ensuring it is seared on all sides.
4. Take out of the pan and put on a plate. Cover in cling film and refrigerate.
5. Now make the sauce, tasting as you go. Add chilli according to preference.
6. Take a sharp knife and finely slice the tuna, arranging it neatly around the plate. Garnish the plate with herb salad or a salad of your choice to give colour and height.
7. Spoon a little teriyaki over the tuna and garnish with a lime wedge.
8. Serve immediately.

Duncan Collinge

Duncan learned his trade from the world-famous Roux brothers and in places as diverse as London's Le Gavroche restaurant and hotels across Europe. He joined Lakeside Hotel, Lake Windermere, 'the best four star hotel in the Lake District' in 1999 and has since become the first chef in Cumbria to be given a Science and Technology Ambassadorship, sharing his experience and enthusiasm to inspire students throughout the Lakes to follow in his footsteps.

Line Caught Cumbrian Sea Bass with Gremolata and Cassoulet of Local Organic Vegetables

Chef Says

This is our local produce at its best - a fresh, 'meaty' fish for a truly mouth-watering dish. This is a real favourite with our guests.

Top tip - always use the freshest fish available to you. If you cannot get wild sea bass then use farmed, but get your fishmonger to fillet it for you. Freezing the gremolata butter will make it last for a couple of months until you make the dish again.

Duncan Collinge
Lakeside Hotel
Lake Windermere
Newby Bridge
Cumbria LA12 8AT
Telephone: 015395 30001
www.Lakesidehotel.co.uk

Serves: 4
Preparation time: 45 minutes
Cooking time:
10 minutes once stock base is done

Ingredients:

Fish
4 x 200g pieces of thick cut sea bass fillets (line caught wild is best)

Gremolata Butter
Zest and juice of 2 lemons
Zest of 1 lime
1/2 bunch of flat parsley
2 cloves of garlic, finely chopped
1 block of local butter

Stock
500g white fish bones
(if you cannot get fish bones then use a vegetable stock cube)
1 glass dry white wine
1/2 leek
1/2 onion
2 sticks celery
1 1/2 pints of water
2 star anise
3 cloves garlic
1/2 bulb fennel
Tarragon stalks
2 bay leaves

Vegetables
8 baby fennel
8 baby carrots
8 baby leeks
Peas and broad beans
Tarragon leaves
8 asparagus spears
8 bok choi leaves

New potatoes optional

Method:

Gremolata Butter
1. Mix the lemon juice, zest, lime, parsley, garlic and butter to a fine paste in a food processor to form a purée. Roll the mixture in cling film into a stick and set in the fridge.

Stock
1. Simmer the bones, white wine, 1/2 leek, 1/2 onion, celery, star anise, garlic, fennel, tarragon stalks and bay leaves roughly chopped with the water in a pan for 20 minutes.
2. Allow to cool. Pass the stock through a muslin cloth or a tea towel and reduce to a pint (follow the same procedure with a vegetable stock cube).

Vegetables
1. Blanch and refresh (cook until just done and plunge into ice water to stop cooking) all vegetables separately apart from the bok choi.
2. When you are ready to serve, reheat the stock adding the fennel, carrots, leeks and asparagus first. Cook for 2 minutes, add the rest and remove from the heat. Divide into 4 bowls.
3. Bring the stock back to boil and whisk in a couple of slices of the gremolata butter.

Fish
1. Pan fry in a non-stick pan for 4-5 minutes skin side down, turn and cook for 2 further minutes, remove and allow to rest for 2 minutes.
2. Place the fish on top of the vegetables and serve with some boiled new potatoes.

48
Dinner Party Menu
Eric Chavot

Appetizer: Minestrone with Pan Fried Herb Gnocchi

Main: Rabbit Provençal with Tomato Risotto

Dessert: Quick and Easy Chocolate Soufflé with Vanilla Ice Cream

Appetizer

Main

Dessert

Eric Chavot

Eric Chavot joined The Capital from Chavot, in London's Fulham Road, where he was Chef/Patron. Previous experience includes Head Chef positions at Interlude de Chavot; The Restaurant (Marco Pierre White), Hyde Park Hotel, and Chez Nico at Ninety, Park Lane. He was also Sous Chef at London's La Tante Claire and Harveys, preceded by Le Manoir aux Quat' Saisons in Great Milton, Oxford. In recognition of his outstanding cuisine, coupled with the exemplary service afforded to visitors to The Capital Restaurant, a second Michelin star was awarded in January 2001.

Appetizer: Minestrone with Pan Fried Herb Gnocchi

Chef Says

I love these recipes as they are typical dishes from my home region of Arcachon in the south of France.

The Capital Hotel
22-24 Basil Street
Knightsbridge
London SW3 1AT
Telephone: 020 7589 5171
www.capitalhotel.co.uk

Try cooking the minestrone with different vegetables according to the season.

Serves: 4
Preparation time: **30 minutes**
Cooking time: **20 minutes**

Ingredients:
Minestrone
50g peeled carrot, diced
50g trimmed leeks, diced
50g courgettes, diced
50g savoy cabbage, diced and blanched
50g sun-dried tomatoes
50g borlotti beans, cooked
50g small tubetti pasta
200g herb gnocchi (see below)
50g pesto
1/2 litre borlotti stock
1/2 litre chicken stock
Extra virgin olive oil
Fresh basil
Salt and pepper

Herb Gnocchi
250g Desirée potato, baked (flesh after being baked)
65g pasta flour
1 egg yolk
25g parmesan, grated
7g chervil, chopped
7g tarragon, chopped
7g flat parsley, chopped
Salt and pepper

Method:
Minestrone
1. Sweat the carrots in olive oil for 3-4 minutes (with a lid on) add the leeks then the courgettes, cook for a further 3-4 minutes. Add the cabbage, and some of the warm stock, bring to a gentle simmer and add the borlotti beans and the tubetti pasta.
2. Set aside and add the pesto and the fresh basil julienne. Check the seasoning and thickness of broth, add more liquid if necessary.

Herb Gnocchi
1. Fold the flour gently with the potato. Add the egg yolk, the parmesan and seasoning. Using a piping bag and a pastry nozzle (size 12), pipe gnocchi mix into a pan with simmering salted water and poach for 3-4 minutes. When cooked cool down in iced water, drain and pat dry on kitchen paper, set aside.
2. Gently pan fry in olive oil in a non-stick pan and sprinkle with grated parmesan.

Above: © Lisa Linder - Condé Nast Traveller

Main: Rabbit Provençal with Tomato Risotto

This recipe also works with chicken. Choose corn fed chickens as they are the best.

Serves: **4**
Preparation time: **30 minutes**
Cooking time: **40 minutes**

Ingredients:

Provençal
4 rabbit legs
100g sun-dried tomato, diced
50g black olives, diced
150g pequillo peppers, diced
1 tablespoon green pesto
100g buffalo mozzarella
Salt and pepper
Olive oil

Tomato Risotto
250g risotto rice
100g onion, finely chopped
3 garlic cloves, crushed
100ml white wine
75ml sherry vinegar
75ml balsamic vinegar
450ml chicken stock or vegetable stock
400ml tomato juice
Thyme
Basil julienne
Parmesan
Mascarpone

Method:

Provençal
1. Sweat the diced peppers in olive oil, season with salt and pepper and a pinch of sugar. Cook for 4-5 minutes, deglaze with sherry vinegar and reduce. Add a dash of balsamic vinegar, reduce and set aside.
2. Off the heat, fold the tomato and olives into the peppers, add the pesto and check the seasoning. Stuff a rabbit leg with provençal mix, sear in olive oil until golden, add a knob of butter and roast in the oven for 8-10 minutes with a clove of garlic and a couple of sprigs of thyme. Leave the leg to rest. Add the rabbit juices to a pan and reduce in consistency. Pour over each leg. Serve with the risotto.

Tomato Risotto
1. Cook the same way as a risotto. Sweat the onion until soft, add the garlic, rice, vinegars and wine. Reduce all the liquid, start to add the hot stock and seasoning. When the rice is cooked add the basil, parmesan and mascarpone.
2. If serving as a risotto cake, over-cook the rice slightly and set in a tray. When cold, cut in whatever shape and wrap in thinly sliced pancetta before pan-frying.
3. Serve with rocket and parmesan salad.

Dessert: Quick and Easy Chocolate Soufflé with Vanilla Ice Cream

You can prepare the soufflé with strawberries instead of chocolate - making it more seasonal for summer.

Serves: 4
Preparation time: **20 minutes**
Cooking time: **30 minutes**
Ice cream must be chilled overnight.

Ingredients:

Soufflé Base:
320g good quality chocolate
200g milk
20g corn flour
60g egg yolks
200g egg white
80g caster sugar

Vanilla Ice Cream
250g milk
2 vanilla pods
3 egg yolks
80g caster sugar
125g double cream

Method:

Soufflé
1. Melt the soufflé chocolate to 50°C. Slowly whisk the egg whites and gradually add the sugar, whisk to a soft peak meringue.
2. Dissolve the corn flour in the cold milk and then bring to the boil, whisking constantly. Cook for 1-2 minutes. Gradually pour the milk onto the chocolate and create an emulsion. Smooth with a hand blender and add the yolks.
3. Fold in the egg whites and spoon into the ramekins. Cook at 190°C for 7-8 minutes. The soufflés can be prepared in advance and refrigerated for up to 4 hours.

Vanilla Ice Cream
1. Bring the milk to the boil with the split vanilla pod, poor gently over the sugar and egg mix (gently folded together). Bring the mix to 63°C, remove from the heat, and add the double cream.
2. Chill overnight for the vanilla pods to release maximum flavour. Churn in your ice cream maker. Pour the cold ice cream inside the hot soufflé. Bon appétit!

52
Dinner Party Menu
Eyck Zimmer

Appetizer: Caramelised Lamb Sweetbreads with Caper and Raisin Chutney

Main: Fillet Steak with Five Onion Sauce and Horseradish Mash

Dessert: Vanilla and Coconut Panna Cotta with Spiced Pineapple Compote

Appetizer

Main

Dessert

Eyck Zimmer

With 40 culinary awards under his belt, Eyck has brought a wealth of experience to the River Restaurant at the Lowry Hotel having worked in some of the best restaurants in the UK, Germany, Switzerland and Portugal. Eyck previously held the position of Head Chef at The Ritz Hotel in London.

Appetizer: Caramelised Lamb Sweetbreads with Caper and Raisin Chutney

Chef Says

Always toast nuts (hazel, pine and almonds) as the high natural oils increase the flavour when toasted.

The Lowry Hotel
50 Dearmans Place
Manchester M3 5LH
Telephone: 0161 827 4000
www.roccofortehotels.com

Serves: 4
Preparation time: 25 minutes
Cooking time: 10 minutes

Ingredients:
12 lamb sweetbread nuggets (20g each)
12 long green asparagus
30g butter
200ml chicken stock
1 bay leaf
1 small carrot, cut in half lengthways
1 small shallot
1 celery stick
40ml oil
80g pine nuts, toasted golden
80g raisins
Zest of 1 lemon, finely grated
20g capers
10g balsamic syrup
100ml olive oil
Salt and pepper
4 portions mixed salad

Method:
1. Soak the sweetbreads in cold water for at least 1 hour.
2. In a pan bring the vegetables and the chicken stock together with the lamb sweetbreads and the bay leaf to boil. After 1 minute quickly place into the freezer.
3. Once cold take off the skin and any white bits.
4. Barb and peel the green asparagus three quarters way down.
5. Cook in rapidly boiling salted water until tender then refresh in ice water and set aside.
6. In a food processor purée the raisins, toasted pine nuts, capers and grated lemon zest to a consistency of a paste, slowly adding the balsamic syrup and olive oil.
7. Adjust seasoning and set aside.
8. When serving, quickly fry the sweetbreads in butter until golden brown and deglaze at the end with some chicken stock. Warm the asparagus and lay in the centre of the plate. Pipe some caper and raisin chutney between each asparagus and place the sweetbreads on top. Garnish with petit salad and serve.

Main: Fillet Steak with Five Onion Sauce and Horseradish Mash

Horseradish and mustard will give the mashed potato a spicy kick and is an excellent flavour combination with the beef.

Serves: 4
Preparation time: 35 minutes
Cooking time: 25 minutes

Ingredients:
4 fillet steaks (180g)
100g leeks, cut into juilienne
100g red onions, thinly sliced
100g shallots, thinly sliced
100g spring onions, sliced
20g chives, chopped
500g potato
50g butter
100ml double cream
40g horseradish, finely grated and kept in cream
60g grain mustard
400g spinach
200ml veal stock
100ml red wine
Salt and pepper

Method:
1. Cook each of the onions and the leek in a little butter with some water. Cook them separately to retain the individual colour. Season with salt and pepper.
2. Set these aside and when serving the steak place a spoon of each different onion in a pot and warm through. Mix in the chopped chives.
3. Roast the steak to your liking.
4. Peel the potatoes and cook in lightly salted water until soft. Make a potato purée in the usual manner with the butter and cream. Finish with the grain mustard and freshly grated horseradish.
5. In a hot pan with some oil, quickly sauté the spinach until soft and then season.
6. To make the red wine sauce, reduce the wine in a pan to a third and add the brown veal stock. Reduce by half and adjust the seasoning.
7. Place the horseradish mash in the centre of the plate and garnish with spinach. Now arrange the fillet steak.
8. Sit a portion of the five onions on top of the steak and drizzle with red wine sauce.

Dessert: Vanilla and Coconut Panna Cotta with Spiced Pineapple Compote

Use Tahitian vanilla as the flavour and quality is the best you can buy. It isn't cheap but it's worth it!

Serves: 4
Preparation time: 25 minutes
Cooking time: 15 minutes

Ingredients:
1 vanilla pod, split lengthways
100ml coconut milk
150ml double cream
2 gelatine leaves
50g caster sugar
150g pineapple
30ml honey
1g cardamom powder
1g star anise powder
1g cinnamon stick
1 pinch nutmeg

Method:
1. In a pan bring the double cream, coconut milk and vanilla to simmer.
2. Add the sugar and dissolve.
3. Soak the gelatine leaves, add to the mixture and dissolve.
4. Stir until it becomes a little creamy and thickens.
5. Pour into chilled glasses three quarters full and refrigerate.
6. To make the spiced pineapple compote, peel and dice the pineapple in $\frac{1}{2}$ cm squares.
7. Heat the honey in a pan and add the diced pineapple and the spices. Quickly stew them without burning for approximately 10 minutes.
8. Set aside and chill.
9. Pour the pineapple mix into the glass on top of the panna cotta and serve.

Gareth Longhurst

Gareth started as a trainee chef in 1988 in Royal Wells Inn, Tunbridge Wells (a 2 rosette restaurant) and left in 1997 as Head Chef. He started with Hotel du Vin in 1998 as Sous Chef at Tunbridge Wells, moving to Winchester where he was Head Chef for 3½ years. He finally moved to Harrogate to open the kitchen in the newly opened hotel in August 2003.

Roasted Monkfish with Curried Crab Velouté

Chef Says

This dish is ideal for dinner parties as you can prepare the fondue and the velouté the day before and keep in the fridge overnight. Then on the day all you have to do is heat through the sauce and cook the fish.

Top tip - always seal fish and meat before cooking in the oven as it keeps all the flavours in.

Hotel Du Vin
Prospect Place
Harrogate
North Yorkshire HG1 1LB
Telephone: 01423 856800
www.hotelduvin.com

Serves: 4
Preparation time: 45 minutes
Cooking time: 10 minutes

Ingredients:
4 x 200g pieces of monkfish tail
250g fresh white crab meat

Tomato Fondue
2 shallots, finely chopped
2 cloves of garlic, crushed
Sprig of thyme
125ml white wine
2 tins chopped tomatoes

Curried Velouté
4 shallots
600ml white wine
600ml fish stock
900ml double cream
1 teaspoon mild curry powder
1 teaspoon tumeric
Chopped dill
¼ of a lemon

Method:
1. Pre-heat oven to 200ºC, 400ºF, Gas Mark 6.

Tomato Fondue
1. Sweat off the chopped shallots and crushed garlic in a little olive oil.
2. Add the thyme and white wine and reduce.
3. Meanwhile, strain the chopped tomatoes.
4. When wine has reduced by three quarters, add the drained tomatoes and simmer until thick.

Curried Velouté
1. Peel and slice the shallots.
2. Put in a thick-bottomed saucepan with the curry powder and tumeric.
3. Add the white wine and reduce by two thirds. Add the fish stock and reduce by half. Add the cream.
4. Bring to the boil and simmer for about 4 minutes.
5. Strain the liquid into a clean saucepan.

To Assemble:
1. Season the monkfish and seal in a frying pan before transferring to a baking sheet and place in a pre-heated oven for 8 minutes.
2. Meanwhile, take the velouté, fondue, crab and mix together. Warm over a moderate heat.
3. Squeeze in a quarter of a lemon and add some chopped dill.
4. Place the crab velouté on a plate and sit the monkfish on top.
5. Serve with green vegetables and potatoes if required.

58
Vegetarian Dinner Party Menu Geoffrey Smeddle

Appetizer: Salad of Beetroot, Goat's Cheese, Fennel and Grain Mustard Vinaigrette

Main: Goan Vegetable Curry

Dessert: Fresh Berries in Elderflower Jelly

Appetizer

Main

Dessert

Geoffrey Smeddle

Geoffrey has a number of accolades to his name including 'Best New Restaurant in Scotland' 2003, 'City Chef of the Year' 2005 and 'AA Restaurant of the Year' 2005-6. He and his wife have just taken over their own restaurant, The Peat Inn, in Fife.

Appetizer: Salad of Beetroot, Goat's Cheese, Fennel and Grain Mustard Vinaigrette

Chef Says

I love the combination of these dishes together as a party menu because they are all bursting with flavour and provide a good hearty meal, but don't leave you feeling like you've eaten more than you should!

Geoffrey Smeddle
The Peat Inn
Peat Inn
Cupar
Fife KY15 5LH
Telephone: 01334 840206
www.thepeatinn.co.uk

I know not everyone is a fan of beetroot but whether in salads, roasted or pickled, I adore it in any shape or form!

Serves: 4
Preparation time: 15 minutes
Cooking time (if cooking beetroot): 1 hour

Ingredients:
4 medium sized beetroot
120g to 140g of goat's cheese, roughly crumbled
1 head fennel
200g mixed salad leaves, washed

Dressing
1 dessertspoon grain mustard
1 teaspoon sugar
$^1/_2$ teaspoon salt
Fresh ground pepper
150ml white wine vinegar
450ml olive oil

Method:
1. Start by cooking the beetroot. You can always buy the pre-cooked variety but if cooking your own, place the beetroots in a pan and cover with cold water, a teaspoon of salt and a glug of red wine vinegar.

2. Bring to a simmer and cook until tender when you insert a knife. Allow to cool in the liquid. When cool enough to touch, peel the skin away with a small knife. It is a good idea to wear rubber gloves when doing this unless you don't mind getting pink stains on your palms! Cut into wedges or diced squares and set aside until later. All this can be done the day before.

3. To make the dressing which can also be done the day before; mix all the ingredients except the oil, in a bowl and whisk thoroughly together. Then slowly drizzle on the oil while whisking well to mix everything together and keep refrigerated until needed.

4. The rest is a simple last minute assembly job. Cut the fennel in half through the root and slice the root out completely. Slice the rest of the fennel into thin slivers, add the leaves and toss all the ingredients in a bowl. Season lightly with salt and add the goat's cheese.

5. Dress the leaves evenly with the dressing and only now add in the beetroot, or it will stain the whole thing red.

6. Arrange in bowls, serve at once, spooning over a little more dressing at the table if you wish.

Main: Goan Vegetable Curry

I'm not a vegetarian myself but still enjoy the satisfaction of creating a tasty vegetarian dish. I like this dish in particular as the Asian influence reminds me of my honeymoon in Thailand.

Serves: 4
Preparation time: 20 minutes
Cooking time: 15 minutes

Ingredients:

4 cups mixed vegetables (potatoes, carrots, cauliflower, french beans), chopped
2 medium onions, chopped
1 inch piece ginger, peeled and chopped
2 cloves garlic, chopped
2 green chillies, chopped
1 teaspoon hot garam masala mix (optional)
1 can unsweetened coconut milk
3 tablespoons melted butter
Salt to taste
Coriander leaves to garnish, finely chopped

Method:

1. Parboil the chopped vegetables and keep aside. Heat half the quantity of butter in a pan on a medium heat until it is hot. Add the chopped onion. Sauté on a medium heat for 4 minutes or until the onions are transparent and soft. Now add the chopped ginger, garlic and green chilli. Stir-fry briefly for a few seconds. Let it cool. Grind this to a fine paste. Keep aside.

2. Heat the remaining quantity of butter in the same pan. Stir-fry the paste you have made for 2 minutes. Now, add the parboiled vegetables and season. Mix well. Cover and cook on medium - low heat for 3 minutes or until the vegetables are fully cooked.

3. Add the garam masala (optional) and the tin of coconut milk. Half fill the empty coconut milk tin with water, swirl the water round to release all the coconut and pour this into the vegetables as well. Simmer on very low heat for about 4 minutes.

4. Garnish with finely chopped coriander leaves.

Dessert: Fresh Berries in Elderflower Jelly

I love the elderflower cordial in this as I find it releases the full flavour of the berries without being over-poweringly sweet. For a more luxurious option use champagne in the jelly; a classic summer combination with strawberries. This looks especially striking if set in champagne or martini glasses.

You can use one type of berry or a selection of berries and currants. The fruit always looks stunning, suspended in the delicate jelly. To give the illusion of berries floating in the jelly, build each layer one at a time, allowing it to set before adding the next. This sounds time consuming, but they set in the fridge in minutes at each stage.

Makes: 4 individual ramekins
Preparation time: 15 minutes
Cooking time: 10 minutes

Ingredients:
50ml unsweetened elderflower cordial
1/2 litre water
6 leaves of gelatine
1/2 a punnet each of your favourite berries, sliced if large.

Method:
1. Mix the cordial and water together, warming it just enough to allow the gelatine to dissolve.
2. Working with the elderflower still warm but not hot, spoon enough elderflower into each ramekin to just cover the bottom, then set in the fridge.
3. When almost set, scatter a layer of berries and spoon in enough elderflower to just cover, allowing this also to set. Continue until the ramekins are full.
4. Allow to set completely in the fridge before turning out. To do this, dip each one in a small bowl of warm water, just to loosen the jelly from the side of the dish.
5. Serve with berries and, for traditionalists, a dollop of cream.

Glen Lester and Dino Pavledis

Forget everything you have ever read or heard about vegetarian food. Forget everything you have ever eaten at vegetarian restaurants. Dining at Terre à Terre is a culinary experience like no other, with intense flavours, sublime textures and a combination of ingredients that few have the imagination or daring to put together.

No. 71

Chef Says

Yuzu juice has a unique citrus flavour. It can be bought from all good oriental suppliers. If you can't get hold of it substitute with lemon and lime juice with a pinch of salt.

Terre à Terre
71 East Street
Brighton BN1 1HQ
Telephone: 01273 729051
www.terreaterre.co.uk

Serves: **4-6**
Preparation time: **1 hour**
Cooking time: **30 minutes**

Ingredients:
Cucumber Granita (make the day before)
¹/₂ cucumber, peeled and deseeded
3 teaspoons pink pickled sushi ginger juice
1 teaspoon mirin
¹/₂ teaspoon wasabi paste
1 pinch salt
100g pickled sushi ginger

Sushi Rice
100g sushi rice
100ml water
25ml sushi vinegar
1 nori sheet
¹/₂ ripe mango

Kohl Rabi
2 kohl rabi
1 fresh lime, juiced
Salt

Shoots and Leaf Salad
1 500g packet of beansprouts
1 punnet shizu cress
1 punnet dakion cress
50g fresh coriander, washed
225ml grape seed oil
Salt and pepper

Method:
Cucumber Granita
1. Blend all apart from the ginger and freeze. When frozen smash with a pestle and mortar, or grate and place in the freezer until needed.
2. Very finely shred pink pickled ginger (some for sushi, some for on top of granita).

Sushi Rice
1. Cover rice and water with a tight lid and bring to fast boil. Once boiling, reduce flame to its lowest possible.
2. When all the water has been absorbed by the rice (takes around 10-12 minutes) remove from heat and leave for 10 minutes to steam.
3. Spread rice onto a tray, mix in the vinegar and allow to cool to room temperature.

4. Toast nori sheets under a low grill until the seaweed changes its green colour.
5. Fine dice the mango.
6. Mix 1 tablespoon of mango and 1 tablespoon of shredded ginger.
7. Place nori sheet rough side up on a rolling mat or cling film will do.
8. Spread rice 2mm thick leaving 1¹/₂cm borders at opposite ends, then place a 3mm ridge of mango and pickle mix across the edge of the rice nearest to you. Slightly dampen one end and roll the nori up pulling the roll back into itself to tighten as you go.
9. Refrigerate. Cut into 2cm long slices and skewer.

Kohl Rabi
1. Peel kohl rabi and slice on a mandolin or with a very sharp knife into see-through slivers.
2. Toss in lime juice and a pinch of salt.
3. Spread out overlapping slices onto cling film, forming 4-6 10cm squares.
4. Store in the fridge until needed.

Shoots and Leaf Salad
1. Cut coriander into 3 (stalks included) and mix gently into cress and beansprouts.
2. Dress with equal quantities of yuzu juice and grape seed oil and season.

To Assemble:
1. Cover the kohl rabi squares with the salad. Roll up pulling tight as you go, lift it out of the cling film and stand on a plate.
2. Rest the sushi skewer on the cress and beansprout salad.
3. Fill a shot glass with granita, sprinkle with ginger shred and serve.

Glynn Purnell

Recently referred to as a 'yummy brummie' by Olive Magazine, Glynn is one of the UK's rising stars. He started cooking professionally at the age of 14 when he took on a job after school and hasn't looked back. Winning dozens of awards including a Michelin star for his inspired, adventurous cooking, he has remained firmly rooted in his home city where he can indulge his passion for local team, Birmingham City FC.

Turbot Poached in Coconut Milk, with Chantenay Carrots cooked in Toffee and Passion Fruit with a Carrot Vinaigrette

Chef Says

Chantenay carrots have a natural sweetness which is complemented by the toffee and passion fruit. The crunchiness of the raw citrusy carrot vinaigrette adds a fabulous contrast that works really well with the creamy coconut flavour of the fish.

Jessica's Restaurant
1 Montague Road
Edgbaston
Birmingham B16 9HN
Telephone: 0121 455 0999
www.glynnpurnell.com

Serves: 2
Preparation time: 15 minutes
Cooking time: 8 minutes

Ingredients:
2 x 150g fillets of turbot
(or you can use brill or sole)
16 Chantenay carrots, trimmed into pyramid shapes, blanched and refreshed (or if you can't find any, large carrots cut into chunks)
1 passion fruit, cut into two and flesh scooped out
1 tin of coconut milk (not half fat version)
110g caster sugar
175g salted butter
Rock salt
Pinch of ground ginger

Carrot Vinaigrette
1 large carrot, peeled and shredded into fine julienne strips
4 teaspoons olive oil
1 teaspoon aged balsamic vinegar
Lemon peel, finely diced

Method:
1. Make the vinaigrette by mixing together all the ingredients and setting to one side.
2. Put coconut milk in a medium pan and bring to a gentle simmer on a low heat.
3. Place the fish in the simmering coconut milk and cook for 3-4 minutes. Then turn off and leave in the coconut milk.
4. Put the sugar into a slightly warmed frying pan and melt until it turns to caramel. Then add the cubed butter and, holding the pan handle, swirl until it turns into toffee.
5. Add the blanched Chantenay carrots and stir until coated in toffee, then add the flesh and seeds of one passion fruit.
6. Using a fish slice, remove the fish from the coconut milk and place on a plate. Season with rock salt and powdered ginger.
7. Add carrots with their caramel on and around the fish.
8. Garnish with carrot vinaigrette.

Gordon Ramsay

Since opening, Gordon Ramsay at Claridge's has enjoyed huge popularity and widespread critical acclaim, including the Tatler 2002 Best Restaurant award and, in January 2003, its first Michelin star. Formerly a professional footballer for Scottish champions Glasgow Rangers, Gordon has become one of the country's most well known faces and his group, Gordon Ramsay Holdings now holds 8 Michelin stars.

Lemon Sole Goujons with Tomato Salsa

Chef Says

Kids will love these baked fish fingers, which offer a healthier alternative to fish and chips, especially when served with a fresh tomato salsa. Japanese panko crumbs are fantastic for giving a crisp coating without needing much oil but you can substitute them for ordinary breadcrumbs if you wish. Just drizzle over a little olive oil before baking.

Top tip - if, like me, you've got more than one pair of tiny hands to keep busy, then give each child a task: one to flour the fish, another to dip them into the egg, a third to breadcrumb them and the fourth to help make the salsa.

Claridges
Brook Street
London W1A 2JQ
Telephone: 020 7499 0099
www.gordonramsay.com

Serves: 4 little ones
Preparation time: 10 minutes
Cooking time: 10 minutes

Ingredients:

Goujons
50g plain flour
Sea salt and freshly ground black pepper
300g skinned sole fillets, sliced into strips
1 large egg, beaten
40-50g panko (or regular) breadcrumbs
Olive oil to drizzle

Tomato Salsa
1 ripe avocado
2 vine-ripened plum tomatoes, chopped
1 small red onion, finely chopped
Juice of 1 lime
3 tablespoons olive oil, plus extra for drizzling
Small handful of coriander, chopped
Pinch of sugar
Sea salt and freshly ground black pepper

Method:

1. Pre-heat the oven to 200ºC, Gas Mark 6. Lightly grease a large baking sheet.
2. Mix the flour and seasoning in a wide bowl. Working in batches, coat the fish strips in the seasoned flour, egg and then breadcrumbs. Arrange in a single layer on the baking sheet.
3. Drizzle the goujons with a little olive oil and bake for about 10 minutes, turning over halfway until the fish is firm and cooked through.
4. Meanwhile, make the salsa. Halve and stone the avocado and use a teaspoon to scoop chunks of flesh into a bowl. Gently mix with the other ingredients and season to taste with salt and pepper.
5. Serve the baked goujons immediately with the tomato sauce.

68
Hugues Marrec

Hugues was born in France, in 1978. With an endless supply of fresh produce from the sea and the land always readily available and a family already passionate about food, Hugues was involved in cooking from a very early age. After training in catering school, Hugues set off to discover other food cultures, travelling to America, French Polynesia and Australia before finally settling down in Kent. From then he has shared his expertise with the team at Rendezvous where he has been Head Chef for the last three years.

Roast Halibut, Caramelised Salsify and Chestnut Mash

Chef Says

I think that in spite of its fantastic qualities, the salsify is a little known and used root vegetable. Its texture and taste complements the halibut perfectly, but it is also lovely with any other fish or poultry.

Rendezvous Brasserie
26 Market Square
Westerham
Kent TN16 1AR
Telephone: 01959 561408
www.rendezvous-brasserie.com

Serves: **4**
Preparation time: **30 minutes**
Cooking time: **12 minutes**

Ingredients:

4 portions of halibut (approx 160g each)
400g salsify
½ cup of balsamic vinegar
20g butter
1 lemon
200g chestnuts, cooked
500ml milk
½ vanilla pod
Drop of white truffle oil
Salt and pepper

Method:

1. Peel and cut the salsify, cover them with water and lemon juice. Add butter, salt, pepper and sugar and bring to the boil.
2. Leave it to simmer until all the liquid has disappeared. Add the vinegar then reduce it again.
3. Cook the chestnut with the vanilla in 250ml of milk for about 15 minutes and then mash it.
4. Cook an extra 100g of salsify in the remaining 250ml of milk then purée, strain and add a few drops of truffle oil. Keep the milk to one side.
5. Cook the halibut skin side down in a non-stick pan for 4 minutes, and then finish in a hot oven for another 4 minutes.

To Serve:

1. Carefully arrange the fish on the top of the salsify, add a spoon of chestnut mash on the side.
2. At the last minute, froth the truffle milk, and add it on the side.
3. Add a few fried salsify sticks to decorate.

Ivano De Serio

In February 2006, The Old Bakery received the 'Lincolnshire Life Best Restaurant of the Year' Award and was the winner in the 'Tastes of Lincolnshire' Restaurant Category. During filming of 'The Da Vinci Code' at Lincoln Cathedral in August 2005, the majority of actors and directors, including Sir Ian McKellen, Audrey Tautou and Ron Howard, dined at the restaurant. They all left personalized messages (such as 'I love the Bakery') in a copy of 'The Da Vinci Code' which has been auctioned to raise money for the local hospital.

Pan Seared Tuna Loin, Caramelised Plantain Carpaccio with Ginger, Lime and Mango Vinaigrette

Chef Says

This recipe is one of my personal favourites from the Cayman Islands where I lived and worked for almost 3 years. It is a dish that can be prepared all year round.

Top tip - serve the tuna rare in the centre to keep the flavour and texture. For ripeness make sure the skin of the plantain is dark yellow and almost brown but still firm to the touch.

The Old Bakery Restaurant
26/28 Burton Road
Lincoln LN1 3LB
Telephone: 01522 576057
www.theold-bakery.co.uk

Serves: 4
Preparation time: 30 minutes
Cooking time: 10 minutes

Ingredients:
300g loin of very fresh blue fin tuna
1 ripe plantain
30g demerara sugar
Toasted sesame oil
10ml vegetable oil
Salt and pepper to taste

Vinaigrette
1 mango
Juice of 3 limes
20ml light soy sauce
30ml vegetable oil
Root of fresh ginger, grated

Method:
1. Cut the loin of tuna in four (like a cross) to obtain four fillets, season with salt, pepper and sesame oil and set aside.
2. Peel and thinly slice the plantain, lay on a well greased tray, sprinkle with salt, pepper and demerara sugar and grill for 1-2 minutes until golden caramelised.
3. For the vinaigrette, peel the mango, place the fruit in a blender, add the soy sauce, ginger, oil and lime juice and blend until smooth.
4. In a hot deep-bottomed non-stick pan, sear the tuna fillets for half a minute each side. To serve, lay the plantain on the plates and with a very sharp knife, slice the tuna. Place onto the carpaccio and drizzle with the vinaigrette.

James Martin

By the age of 12, James was able to say that he'd cooked for the Queen Mother at Castle Howard. At 21 he opened the Hotel Du Vin and Bistro in Winchester as Head Chef and was so successful that there was an 8 week waiting list for a table! Since first appearing on TV in November 1996 he's rarely been off screen, most recently starring in the BBC show 'Strictly Come Dancing'. He is most well known for his appearances on the popular daytime programme 'Ready, Steady, Cook', where he is still a regular.

Marshmallows

Chef Says

Bonfire Night has to be the best night of the year for me as: a) I get a day off b) I get to eat marshmallows toasted on the open fire and c) there's that warm and cold feeling in the air.

Top tip - make sure that all the equipment when making marshmallows is very clean. Marshmallows will keep great in an airtight container. If you want pink ones just add red food colouring whilst whisking when cooling.

www.jamesmartinchef.co.uk

Preparation time: 45 minutes
Cooking time:
For the sugar: 15 minutes
In the machine: 15 minutes
Total time: 30 minutes

Ingredients:
455g granulated sugar
1 tablespoon liquid glucose
9 sheets of gelatine
2 egg whites, size 1
1 teaspoon vanilla extract
Icing sugar
Cornflour

Method:
1. Put the granulated sugar, glucose and 200ml water in a heavy-based saucepan. Bring to the boil and continue cooking until it reaches 127°C, 260°F on a sugar thermometer.
2. Meanwhile, soak the gelatine in 140ml cold water. Beat the egg whites until stiff. When the syrup is up to temperature, carefully place the softened gelatine sheets and their soaking water into the sugar. The syrup will bubble up so keep an eye on it. Pour the syrup into a metal jug.
3. Continue to beat the egg whites (preferably with an electric whisk) while pouring in the hot syrup from the jug. The mixture will become shiny and start to thicken. Add the vanilla extract and continue whisking for about 5-10 minutes, until the mixture is stiff and thick enough to hold its shape on the whisk.
4. Lightly oil a shallow baking tray, about 30 x 20cm (12 x 8 inches). Dust it with sieved icing sugar and cornflour then spoon the mixture over and smooth it with a wet palette knife if necessary.
5. Leave for at least an hour to set. Dust the work surface with more icing sugar and cornflour. Loosen the marshmallow around the sides of the tray with a palette knife then turn it out on to the dusted surface. Cut into squares and roll in the sugar and cornflour. Leave to dry a little before packing them into an airtight box.

74
Dinner Party Menu
Jean Christophe Novelli

Appetizer: Pan Fried Boudin Noir and Seared Diver Caught Scallops with Chargrilled Belle de Fontany Potatoes

Main: Monkfish Cheeks and Braised Pig's Cheeks with a Carrot and Cardamom Mash

Dessert: Grenadine Braised Rhubarb and Vanilla Bourbon Panna Cotta

Appetizer

Main

Dessert

Jean Christophe Novelli

Michelin star winning Jean-Christophe Novelli, who starred in 'Hell's Kitchen' and 'Celebrity X Factor', is director of the internationally recognised Novelli Academy, with master classes by himself and other celebrity chefs. He has now created exciting new menus for his new project 'A Touch of Novelli', the first of which features the White Horse in Harpenden, Hertfordshire - not far from his cookery school.

Appetizer: Pan Fried Boudin Noir and Seared Diver Caught Scallops with Chargrilled Belle de Fontany Potatoes

Chef Says

The marriage of flavours, textures and colours makes this an impressive dish and the perfect start to your dinner party!

The White Horse
Hatching Green
Harpenden
Hertfordshire AL5 2JP
Telephone: 01582 713428
www.jeanchristophenovelli.com

Serves: 2
Preparation time: 15 minutes
(apples should be made the day before and stored in an airtight container).
Cooking time: 30 minutes

Ingredients:

6 slices black pudding
4 medium scallops, cut in half
50g Belle de Fontany Potatoes
1 Granny Smith apple
10g horseradish
40ml cream
1 lemon, juiced
5ml vinegar
30ml groundnut oil
2 concassé tomatoes
50g roquette leaves
5g chervil
5g dill
5g tarragon
5g flat parsley
Seasoning

Method:

1. Slice the black pudding and keep it in the fridge until required.
2. Prepare the scallops by removing from the shells. Trim the roe to leave the scallops clean and wash.
3. Boil the potatoes in water until just cooked. Remove and leave to stand.
4. Peel the potatoes and slice into nice even rounds. Chargrill to leave nice bar markings and reserve in oil until serving.
5. Cut the apple into very thin slices across the middle and brush with stock syrup on both sides. Place on a baking sheet lined with greaseproof paper and put into the oven on 150ºC, Gas Mark 2 for 30 minutes until the apple has dried out. Put aside.
6. Peel the horseradish and grate on a fine grater. Add the cream and season with salt and lemon juice.
7. Pan-fry the scallops and black pudding until nicely golden brown.
8. Mix the roquette and concasse with the apple slices. Dress the herb salad.
9. Arrange 5 grilled potatoes on a round plate and add 3 pan-fried scallops and 3 black pudding slices. Dress with the apple slices. Place the salad in the centre and serve immediately.

Main: Monkfish Cheeks and Braised Pig's Cheeks with a Carrot and Cardamom Mash

If you can't get monkfish try turbot or scallops.

Serves: **4**
Preparation time: **40 minutes**
Cooking time: **1½ hours**

Ingredients:
8 monkfish cheeks (ask your fishmonger)
8 pig's cheeks (ask your butcher)
150ml red wine
150ml port
120g butter
200g mixed carrot, celery and onion, roughly diced
150ml veal stock

Carrot and Cardamom Mash
2 large carrots, cut into chunks
1 teaspoon sugar
2 garlic cloves, peeled
2 tablespoons olive oil
A handful of parsley, chopped
½ lemon, juice only
2 cardamom pods, cracked

Method:
1. Marinate the pig's cheeks in the wine and port, preferably overnight. Drain and reserve the liquor. Dry thoroughly.
2. Brown the meat in half of the butter then brown the diced carrot, celery and onion in the remainder and combine in a heavy pot. Add the reserved liquor and veal stock and braise in the oven for 1½ hours at 150ºC.

Carrot and Cardamom Mash
1. Place cardamom pods in a saucepan with water and bring to the boil. Top and tail the carrots but do not peel them. Place a colander into the pan of simmering water but do not let it touch the water. Place carrots into the colander and steam for approximately 15 minutes until tender.
2. Remove from the heat and mash with the sugar, garlic, olive oil, parsley and lemon juice.

To serve:
1. Warm the carrot mash in a little butter.
2. At the same time in another pan warm the pig's cheeks in some of the braising liquor.
3. Pan-fry the monkfish cheeks in a little olive oil until golden in colour (3-4 minutes).
4. Place 4 spoonfuls of mash onto a plate and then place 2 monkfish cheeks and 2 pig's cheeks onto the mash. Garnish with chervil.

Dessert: Grenadine Braised Rhubarb and Vanilla Bourbon Panna Cotta

The champagne and sugar used in this dessert gives the rhubarb a lovely sweet flavour. It's a light, refreshing alternative to the more traditional rhubarb crumble.

Serves: **4**
Preparation time: **30 minutes**
Cooking time: **8 hours including setting time**

Ingredients:

Braised Rhubarb
250g rhubarb
100g sugar
200ml champagne
50ml grenadine
1 vanilla pod (split)

Rhubarb Jelly
9g gelatine leaves
½ litre rhubarb cooking liquor

Panna Cotta
½ pt double cream
¼ pt full fat milk
20g caster sugar
10g gelatine leaf
1 vanilla pod

Method:

Braised Rhubarb
1. Place all ingredients onto a baking tray and braise for 30 minutes at 160°C. Drain, keeping the liquor to one side.

Rhubarb Jelly
1. Soak the gelatine in cold water until soft.
2. Bring the liquor to the boil and whisk the softened gelatine in until completely dissolved.
3. Cool down in a bowl over ice until cold and place into glasses.
4. Leave to set in the fridge for 3-4 hours.

Panna Cotta
1. Add all the ingredients except the gelatine into a pan and bring to the boil.
2. Place the gelatine into cold water until soft.
3. Whisk the softened gelatine into the cream until dissolved.
4. Pass through a sieve and cool in a bowl over ice.
5. When cool pour on top of the set jelly and leave to set for 3-4 hours.

To Serve:
1. Place some of the braised rhubarb on top of the panna cotta and garnish with fresh mint.

Jose Luis Hermosa

With experience from all over Spain, Jose, 'The Chef from Jerez', whose family own a Michelin rated restaurant, was lured to La Tasca five years ago. With its authentic Spanish atmosphere and ingredients La Tasca provides the ideal palette for this culinary artist to create a real taste of Spain for all to savour.

Paella de Marisco

Chef Says

This is a classic Spanish dish, ideal for family and friends to enjoy together on any occasion!

The beauty of this dish is that it is so rich in ingredients and flavours that no other food is required to accompany it. It is best enjoyed with a lovely cool bottle of white wine or pitcher of sangria!

Top tip - simply replace the fish with seasonal vegetables and substitute the stock for a vegetable one and you have a great vegetarian dish. For meat lovers, the fish may be replaced by chorizo (Spanish sausage) and chicken, and the fish stock with chicken stock.

La Tasca
14-16 Bridge Street
Cambridge CB2 1UF
Telephone: 01223 464630
www.latasca.co.uk

Serves: 4 hungry people or 6 with smaller appetites!
Preparation time: 20 minutes
Cooking time: 40 minutes

Ingredients:

15ml olive oil
1 medium onion, finely diced
½ red and ½ green pepper, finely chopped
1 clove of garlic, crushed
1 small tin (250g) chopped tomatoes
800ml fish stock
300g short grain (paella) rice
½ teaspoon saffron
125g squid rings
125g peeled king prawns, uncooked
Mussels in full shells, uncooked
125g monkfish, chopped
125g raw tuna, chopped
4 raw langoustines
4 raw tiger prawns
Season with a sprinkle of salt
¼ of a lemon per person (lemon wedge!)
Handful of parsley, freshly chopped

Method:

1. Heat the oil over a medium heat in a paella pan. Add the onions, peppers and garlic and soften for about 5 minutes.
2. Add the tomatoes, squid, tuna, king prawns and monkfish and fry for 5 minutes until the fish looks cooked on the outside.
3. Add the rice and a sprinkle of salt and sauté for a further 2 minutes until the rice becomes slightly clear.
4. Add the stock and saffron. Gently mix all the ingredients together and bring to the boil whilst stirring gently.
5. Once boiling turn the heat down to low and leave to simmer for about 15 minutes. Gently shake the pan every 5 minutes to avoid sticking but don't stir.
6. Most of the stock, but not all, should now be absorbed. Garnish the top of the paella with the langoustines and tiger prawns and all round the edges with mussels, then place in a medium heat oven for 10 minutes. If necessary, add a little bit more water at this stage to avoid the rice at the top from drying out.
7. Remove from the oven and check all the liquid is absorbed. Try a little bit of the rice to ensure that it is all thoroughly cooked through. If the rice still needs a bit more cooking time add a splash more water and return to the oven for another 5 minutes.
8. Repeat the above process until you are happy with the results! Allow to settle for about 5 minutes.
9. Garnish with lemon wedges and sprinkle with fresh parsley. Serve straight from the pan onto individual plates with a wedge of fresh lemon on each plate. Beware as the pan will be VERY HOT!

BUEN PROVECHO! (Enjoy your meal!)

Kevin Woodford

Kevin's relaxed style, immense skill and ability to communicate at all levels brought him acclaim on 'The Reluctant Cook', 'Big Kevin Little Kevin', 'Ready Steady Cook' and 'Can't Cook, Won't Cook', for which he was voted Best Daytime Television Presenter at 'The National Television Awards'.

Summer Fruit Crunch Slice

Chef Says

This pudding incorporates the lightest of cakes with the sweetest of summer fruits, topped with an 'explode in the mouth' crunchy topping. Use whatever soft summer fruits are available, but it is also really lovely with a selection of exotic fruits such as mango and passion fruits.

www.kevinwoodford.com

Serves: 4
Preparation time: **20 minutes**
Cooking time: **8-10 minutes**

Ingredients:

3 eggs
150g caster sugar
75g plain flour
1½ teaspoons baking powder
Pinch of salt
15g unsalted butter
2 tablespoons golden syrup
175g mixed summer soft fruits
1 small glass Grand Marnier, Cointreau or Kirsch
225g crème fraiche

Method:

1. Whisk the eggs with 75g of the caster sugar until the mixture doubles in size.
2. Sift the flour, ½ teaspoon of baking powder and a pinch of salt onto the egg mixture. Using a metal spoon cut all the dry ingredients into the egg mixture until blended. Transfer to a greaseproof paper-lined Swiss roll tin and bake for 8-10 minutes in a pre-heated oven at 220ºC, Gas Mark 7 until golden and just cooked.
3. Put 50g of the caster sugar, the unsalted butter and golden syrup in a pan and heat gently, stirring until the sugar dissolves. Increase the heat and cook without stirring until the mixture turns golden brown, then mix through 1 teaspoon of baking powder.
4. Pour the mixture onto a baking tray ensuring that it spreads evenly. Cover with greaseproof paper and leave to cool.
5. Remove the cake from the oven and turn it out onto a surface that has been lightly covered with caster sugar. Take off the paper and cut the cake into three pieces.
6. Mix the fruits with the liqueur and crème fraiche and cover the top of each cake with some of the fruit mixture.
7. Break the sugar honeycomb into small pieces and sprinkle over the fruit on the cake. Place the cakes on top of each other and serve.

Lesley Waters

As well as her regular appearances on 'Ready Steady Cook', Lesley has also presented 'Can't Cook, Won't Cook' and made guest appearances on 'Food & Drink' and 'Who'll Do the Pudding?' She's also written several cook books and currently hosts cookery days at her home in Dorset.

Banana and Cinnamon Whirls

Chef Says

This is an adaptation of traditional Chelsea buns, a favourite of mine when I was training to be a chef. It's now a firm favourite with my children, who look for any excuse to make bread dough! As they don't like currants or sultanas, we use bananas instead, which they love.

Top tip - to knead the bread push down into the dough with the heel of your hand, pushing away from you folding the dough as you go. Repeat this for about 10 minutes.

www.lesleywaters.com

Makes: 9 whirls
Preparation time: 30 minutes plus rising time
Cooking time: 20-25 minutes

Ingredients:
Basic Granary Bread Dough
Makes 2 batches
225g strong white flour
225g malted granary bread flour
1 teaspoon salt
1 teaspoon caster sugar
7g sachet of easy blend yeast
150ml warm milk
1 egg, beaten
1 tablespoon olive oil
100-150ml warm water

Buns
1/2 batch basic granary bread dough
25g unsalted butter, melted
2 medium bananas
100g dried apricots, chopped
1 teaspoon cinnamon
50g light muscovado sugar
Zest of 1/2 orange
2 tablespoons runny honey

Method:
Basic Granary Bread Dough
1. Mix the flours and salt together in a large bowl then stir in the sugar and yeast. Make a well in the centre of the flour and pour in the warm milk, beaten egg, olive oil and enough of the water to form a soft, wet dough.
2. On a lightly floured surface, knead dough for 10 minutes until smooth. Put the dough in a lightly oiled bowl, cover with oiled cling film, then leave to rise in a warm place until doubled in size.

3. Split the dough into two. Set half aside for buns. Knead the other half briefly to punch out any air from rising and wrap in cling film. This can be kept in the freezer for up to one month.

Buns
1. Lightly butter a 20cm square baking tin. On a floured surface, roll the dough into a rectangle approximately 30cm x 25cm and brush with melted butter.
2. Thinly slice the bananas into a bowl and mix with the apricots, sugar, cinnamon and orange zest. Spoon mix over the dough, leaving a finger-width border.
3. Roll the dough towards you from the long side of the rectangle, tucking in any banana that falls out. Press ends together to seal. With a sharp knife, cut into 9 pieces and place, cut side up, in the tin, just touching each other. Cover loosely with oiled cling film and set aside in a warm place to rise for 30 minutes.
4. Heat oven at 200°C, Fan 180°C, Gas Mark 6. Warm the honey in a pan or in the microwave on high for 5 seconds, then brush half over the buns. Bake for 20-25 minutes until golden. Allow to cool in the tin for 10 minutes before removing to a cooling rack. Brush with the remaining honey then pull apart to serve.

Lucy Nicholson

Lucy's of Ambleside was born through a love of food and dedication to both the local and visitor population of Ambleside and its surrounding area. This fabulous combination of delicatessen, café and restaurant, outside catering and wine bar and bistro nestles in the heart of the English Lake District. Lucy's most recent addition is her cookery school, which opened earlier this year to inspire, educate and above all entertain by putting the 'oo' back into food.

Roast Leg of Lakeland Lamb

Chef Says

The combination of this beautiful Herdwick with Lyth Valley damsons and Cumberland rum butter, quite simply represents everything that I love about the Lake District and reminds me how fortunate we are to have so many glorious foods on our doorstep in Cumbria.

Top tip - if you are unable to obtain damsons, then why not try a Cumberland sauce instead?

Lucy's of Ambleside
Church Street
Ambleside
The Lake District
Cumbria LA22 0BU
Telephone: 015394 32288
www.lucysofambleside.co.uk

Serves: 4-6 Cumbrian appetites!
Preparation time: 15 minutes max!
Cooking time: Allow 25 minutes per 450g plus 25 minutes

Ingredients:

1.25kg lean leg of Herdwick from Yew Tree Farm, Coniston (www.heritagemeats.co.uk)
100g butter, softened
2 pinches nutmeg
25g soft brown sugar (caster will do if you don't have soft brown)
Zest of 1 lemon plus half the juice
200g Lyth Valley (or similar quality) damsons - remove the stones or tell your guests that you don't wish to have a dental bill if they crack their teeth!!
100ml rum (any will do - although dark rum is best!)

Method:

Lamb

1. Set your oven to 180°C, 350°F, Gas Mark 4. Place the Herdwick onto a rack in a roasting tin and roast in the oven for approximately 1¼ hours.

Rum Butter

1. While it is cooking, combine the butter, sugar, nutmeg, lemon and 2 good tablespoons of the rum.
2. Spread the rum butter over the lamb and return to the oven for the final ½ hour of cooking.

Lyth Valley Damson Sauce

1. During this time put the damsons and the remaining rum in a saucepan and simmer for approximately 15 minutes until it has reduced.

To Serve:

1. Remove the lamb from the oven, cover with greaseproof paper or a cloth and allow it to rest for approximately 15 minutes.
2. Carve and serve with new potatoes, seasonal vegetables and the damson sauce.

Matthew Smith

From as far back as Matthew can remember he loved making and experimenting with food. As a young boy he enjoyed spending time in the kitchen with his mum - learning the basics, baking cakes and licking the spoon. As Executive Head Chef for Orient-Express in the UK, Matthew tells us that "Seeing others enjoy the dishes I prepare fuels my passion for cooking. I love being a part of making someone's special occasion extraordinary, which is a big element of my job at Orient-Express".

Roasted Fillet of Lamb, Celeriac and Chive Mash served with a Tomato and Chilli Jam

Chef Says

This is one of my favourite recipes as it has a variety of textures and flavours and looks extremely delectable.

Top tip - the tomato and chilli jam can be made a day in advance and kept in the fridge until needed.

The Orient-Express
British Pullman and
Northern Belle
Telephone: 0845 077 2222
www.orient-express.com

Serves : 4
Preparation time: 20 minutes
Cooking time: 20-30 minutes

Ingredients:

4 portions of lamb fillet (140g-160g), larder trimmed
2 heads of celeriac, peeled and quartered
10g butter
1 bunch of chives, chopped
1 onion, peeled and sliced
1 red pepper, peeled and sliced
1 red chilli, de-seeded and finely diced
10g ginger, peeled and crushed
1 clove of garlic, peeled and crushed
1 punnet cherry tomatoes, halved
10g caster sugar
10ml fish sauce
Salt and pepper
Small measure of port
200ml lamb stock

Method:

1. Heat a small roasting tray with a little olive oil, add the celeriac and roast in the oven at 180°C for 20 minutes.
2. While the celeriac is roasting, sweat the pepper, onions, chilli, garlic and ginger in olive oil in a pan on top of the stove for about 10 minutes, until soft.
3. Add the cherry tomatoes, sugar and fish sauce and cook for about 20 minutes until the mixture becomes a jam. Keep stirring this all the time to ensure the mixture does not catch the bottom of the pan.
4. When the celeriac is soft, remove it from the oven and mash it. Add the butter, seasoning and the chopped chives.
5. Seal the lamb in a hot pan, season with salt and freshly ground black pepper and cook in the oven at 180°C for 10-12 minutes.
6. Take the lamb out to rest and de-glaze the pan with the port. Add the lamb stock, reduce and skim.
7. Place the celeriac and chive mash in the centre of a plate, slice the fillet of lamb and arrange on the mash. Spoon the tomato and chilli jam on top, pour the sauce around the lamb and mash. Serve with seasonal vegetables.

Win a journey on the
Orient-Express
with
This is my favourite...

see page
160

88
Dinner Party Menu
Michael Caines MBE

Appetizer: Vegetable and Herb Soup

Main: Seafood Risotto

Dessert: Caramelised Lemon Tart with Crème Chantilly

Appetizer

Main

Dessert

Michael Caines MBE

Michael Caines is one of Britain's highest profile chefs and has held two Michelin stars since 1999. He came to Gidleigh Park to take up the position of Head Chef in 1994, a position he has held ever since, winning many accolades and awards. Most recently, Michael took part in the BBC Two series 'Great British Menus', where he was challenged to cook a banquet for the Queen's 80th birthday celebrations in June 2006.

Appetizer: Vegetable and Herb Soup

Chef Says

This is a simple and wonderful soup for the summer; full of flavour yet light and fresh. If you are vegetarian then simply replace the chicken stock with water. The vegetable dice doesn't have to be exact, but make sure it's even, so that you get even cooking through the vegetables.

Top tip - you can use different types of herbs to introduce different flavours, and enhance the soup, but make sure they are fresh herbs and added at the last moment so they remain fresh in colour and flavour.

Michael Caines
Gidleigh Park
Chagford
Devon TQ13 8HH
Telephone: 01647 432367
www.gidleigh.com
www.michaelcaines.com

Serves: 4/5
Preparation time: 20 minutes
Cooking time: 40 minutes

Ingredients:

20g shallots, finely chopped
35g leeks, 10mm diced
50g carrots, 10mm diced
50g courgettes, 10mm diced
50g celeriac, 10mm diced
50g cabbage, 10mm diced
50g peas
50g French beans
50g tomatoes, blanched and seeded, 10mm diced
50ml white wine
500ml water or 500ml chicken stock
12 basil leaves, chopped roughly
5g sorrel, chopped roughly
5g chervil, chopped roughly
5g chives, chopped
100g cream
150g unsalted butter
Pinch of sugar
Salt and pepper

Method:

1. Sweat the shallots, leeks, celeriac and carrots with 25g of butter and a pinch of salt for 5 minutes. Do not brown.
2. Add the white wine and boil until reduced to nothing, add the water and chicken stock and bring to the boil.
3. Cook out for about 10 minutes. Add the courgettes, French beans, peas and cabbage and cook for a further 5 minutes.
4. Now add the cream and whisk in the butter. Add the herbs and tomato and season with salt, pepper and a pinch of sugar. Enjoy!

Main: Seafood Risotto

Risotto can be an easy thing to do well but a hard thing to get right, as the cooking of the rice can spoil the dish if too al dente (crunchy) or over-cooked. It is also a good way of using up offcuts and small pieces of fish. In this recipe I have chosen to use red mullet, sea bass, scallops and king prawns but you can use any types of fish, or indeed just one type of fish, for this dish to work. Alternative herbs can also be used, for example basil or tarragon instead of dill.

Serves: 8
Preparation time: 10 minutes
Cooking time: 40 minutes

Ingredients:

400g scallops, cut in half
400g red mullet, filleted and cut into large pieces
300g sea bass, cut into large pieces
100g king prawns
Parmesan, freshly grated
Fresh dill, chopped

Risotto Base
400g arborio risotto rice
100g onion, diced small
100g fennel, diced small
100g carrot, diced small
100ml extra virgin olive oil
600ml fish stock
600ml water
1 clove garlic, crushed
Pinch of saffron
Salt and pepper

Method:

1. In a flat-bottomed pan, sweat the onions, fennel, carrot and garlic in the olive oil with a pinch of salt and pepper. Add the saffron and then the rice and seal well.
2. Gradually add the hot fish stock, stirring continuously, and cook for 18 minutes.
3. Add the pieces of scallops and prawn and continue to cook, stirring carefully. Once the fish is cooked, add the grated parmesan and chopped dill and stir in well.
4. Pan fry the mullet and sea bass skin side down in olive oil, serve the fish risotto into bowls and then garnish with the pan-fried fish.

Dessert: Caramelised Lemon Tart with Crème Chantilly

Plan ahead! This pastry must be prepared in advance, wrapped in cling film and refrigerated for at least 2 hours before using.

Serves: 12
Preparation time: 40 minutes (plus 2 hours chilling time)
Cooking time: 15-20 minutes at 160°C

Ingredients:

Sweet Pastry
250g butter
175g icing sugar
3 eggs
1 pinch of salt
Zest of 1 orange
500g flour, sieved
Parchment paper
Baking beans

Lemon Cream
380g lemon juice
12 egg yolks
6 eggs
300g sugar
250g butter

Crème Chantilly
150g whipping cream
20g icing sugar

Method:

Sweet Pastry

1. In a mixing bowl cream together the butter and the icing sugar until white, using a hand blender or whisk.
2. Add the sieved flour, orange and salt and bring the mix to a sandy crumble.
3. Add little-by-little the eggs, then bring the mix together on the first speed and once the mix is firm remove from the machine.
4. Wrap in cling film and refrigerate for at least 2 hours before using.

After 2 hours

5. Butter a tart ring and place onto a flat-bottomed tray.
6. Roll out the pastry evenly and line the tin using a piece of pastry to ensure that the corners are well pressed into the bottom.
7. Leave the excess overhanging the edge then line with parchment paper before filling with baking beans to the top.
8. Bake for 10 minutes in the pre-heated oven and then remove. Using a sharp serrated knife, cut away the top of the excess pastry. Return to the oven and continue to bake for a further 10 minutes.
9. Remove the beans and paper and place back into the oven to ensure the base is dry for a minute. Leave to cool before filling with the hot lemon cream.

Lemon Cream

1. Bring the lemon juice to the boil in a saucepan.
2. Cream together the egg yolks, eggs and sugar then add a small amount of the hot lemon juice.
3. Whisk together until smooth and add the remaining lemon juice.
4. Bring back to the boil, whisking all the time until smooth.
5. Remove from the heat and place into a blender. Add the butter progressively and blend until smooth.
6. Pour into the pre-baked tart and leave to set in the fridge.

Crème Chantilly

1. Sift the icing sugar into the cream and whip to a peak.
2. Leave in the fridge until needed.

To Serve:

1. Remove the ring from the tart and cut the tart into the required portion size.
2. Dust lightly with icing sugar.
3. Using a blow lamp, caramelise the icing sugar lightly and leave to cool.
4. Spoon on some Crème Chantilly and enjoy!

92
Michael Duff

Michael beat 5,871 other entrants from 581 schools throughout the UK to be crowned winner of FutureChef 2006, a nationwide competition run by the Springboard Charitable Trust. Michael first took a shine to cooking when he was seven years old and was taken to the Ideal Home Exhibition where he was invited on stage to do a cooking demonstration with Eric de Blond. His mum, Liz can still remember having to buy all the ingredients for Michael to cook the dish at home!

Tagliatelle of Bitter Sweet Orange Pancakes with Hot Dark Chocolate Sauce

Chef Says

I love the flavour of the bitter sweet oranges as they complement the chocolate sauce, and the three orange flavours really give the dish some depth.

FutureChef 2006
Telephone: Springboard
Charitable Trust and
Springboard UK Ltd
020 7395 9496
www.springboarduk.org.uk

Serves: **2**
Preparation time: **20 minutes**
Cooking time: **30 minutes**

Ingredients:
110g plain flour
1 tablespoon caster sugar
1 egg, beaten
350ml semi-skimmed milk
4 oranges
25g unsalted butter, melted
1 clove
50g caster sugar
10g unsalted butter, cubed
75g dark chocolate
50ml double cream
Dash of milk
Cube of butter
Oil for pancakes

Method:
1. Zest three of the oranges for the pancake batter.
2. In a bowl add the flour, the tablespoon of caster sugar and the zest. Make a well in the centre and slowly pour in the beaten egg and melted butter and whisk. Gradually pour in the milk until the mixture is thin and loose (you may not need all the milk).
3. Segment two oranges and place them on a jay cloth. Juice the other two oranges and add the juice to a saucepan with 50g caster sugar and a crushed clove. Reduce to a syrup on a low heat.
4. Heat a tablespoon of vegetable oil in a pancake pan and make six pancakes. Leave to cool (but do not put them in the fridge).
5. Place the chocolate, double cream and a dash of milk in a bain-marie until melted.
6. Check the orange sauce and run through a chinois into a smaller pan and keep warm.
7. Test the consistency of the chocolate sauce and when runny pour into a squeezy bottle.
8. On a baking tray, take a blow torch to one side of the orange segments until slightly blackened, slice them in half, trimming the edges.
9. Trim the pancakes and slice evenly, to resemble tagliatelle. Monte the butter through the orange sauce, to taste and keep warm. Warm the 'tagliatelle' pancakes through in the microwave for about 15 seconds.

To Serve:
1. Make a nest of 'tagliatelle' pancakes in the centre of the bowl. Scatter the seared orange segments over the top. Spoon the orange syrup over the pancakes and drizzle with a little chocolate sauce to finish.

Michael Knight

Michael left his native Wales at the age of nineteen to become a Head Chef of the Royal Corinthian Yacht Club, Isle of Wight. He moved back to Wales sixteen years later to open his first restaurant. His self-taught style and use of the freshest Welsh produce makes Knights Restaurant one of the busiest in Wales. It is not uncommon to rub shoulders with A-list stars at Knights, including fellow countrywoman Catherine Zeta-Jones and her husband Michael Douglas.

Spicy Duck and King Prawns

Chef Says

A great all-year-round dish, simple to prepare and quick to cook, ideal for spending more time with your guests.

Top tip - If you are using frozen king prawns, peel them when they are semi-frozen.

Knights Restaurant
614-618 Mumbles Road
Mumbles
Swansea SA3 4EA
Telephone: 01792 363184

Serves: **4**
Preparation time: **15 minutes**
Cooking time: **10-12 minutes**

Ingredients:
2 large Gressingham duck breasts
16 large fresh or frozen king prawns
2 red peppers
2 red onions
1 large tablespoon fresh ginger, chopped
½ large tablespoon fresh garlic, chopped
2 mild red chillies, chopped
2 large tablespoons light soy sauce
2 large tablespoons medium sherry
1 large tablespoon sesame oil
275ml of passata sauce
1 bunch coriander

Method:
1. Remove the skin from each duck breast and cut into 6 strips.
2. Peel the king prawns and set aside. Cut the peppers and the red onions into ½ inch cubes.
3. Heat a large frying pan until hot and add 20ml of vegetable oil, add the peppers, onions and duck strips. Cook for 2 minutes on each side, then turn temperature down to a medium heat.
4. Add chopped garlic, chilli and ginger and cook for a further minute.
5. Place the soy sauce, sesame oil, sherry and passata in the frying pan and cook for a further 2 minutes.
6. Finally add the king prawns and coriander and cook slowly for a further 3-5 minutes.
7. Serve with jasmine rice and a sprig of fresh coriander.

Michel Roux

Michel has been Chef de Cuisine at Le Gavroche, London since 1991. Le Gavroche became the first UK restaurant to be awarded three Michelin stars.

Savoie Salad

Chef Says

The Savoie salad is a classic dish from the Alpine mountains of the Savoie region of France. Classic combinations like this are hard to beat. Increase the ingredients and this could make a light lunch as well as a starter.

Le Gavroche
43 Upper Brook Street
London W1K 7QR
Telephone:
020 7408 0881 / 020 7499 1826
www.le-gavroche.co.uk

Serves: 6
Preparation time: **15 minutes**
Cooking time: **30 minutes**

Ingredients:
750g Mâche salad leaves (lamb's lettuce)
6 salad potatoes
(Charlotte or Belle de Fontenay)
2 shallots, peeled and thinly sliced
200g air-dried, lightly smoked bacon cut
into lardons - 20mm x 5mm
Olive oil
Walnut oil
Red wine vinegar
Salt and pepper
300g Comte, Gruyère or Beaufort cheese

Method:
1. Cook the washed potatoes in salted boiling water. When cool enough to handle, peel and slice thinly. Drizzle with a little walnut oil, season then cover and keep warm.
2. In a pan, gently fry the lardons with a smear of olive oil. The lardons should be crispy but not dry, add a few drops of vinegar and pour all of this into the potatoes.
3. Dress the well-washed salad with a little walnut oil, vinegar, salt and pepper. Add the shallots and then the warm potato mix.
4. Finally, sprinkle over shavings of the cheese. Serve warm.

Mitchell Tonks

Mitchell Tonks is founder of the award winning FishWorks chain of fishmongers, restaurants and cookery schools. His career in food and seafood has been driven by an honest passion to enthuse, cook for and inspire others to enjoy seafood. He was voted Restaurateur of the Year in 2006 by Tatler and his book, 'The Fishmonger's Cookbook' won the World Gourmand award in 2005 - testament to Mitch's hard work and inspiration.

Spaghetti with Seafood, Fresh Tomato, Olive Oil and Parsley

Chef Says

This is a great dish. It makes the best of everything that you might expect to find at your fishmongers. Be flexible; pretty much any fish or shellfish is fine (except mackerel and other oily fish such as tuna and perhaps salmon). I've used a lot of different species but you can use just one or two things if you'd prefer. Instead of using fresh tomatoes you could just add some fresh tomato sauce.

FishWorks
Bath, Bristol, Christchurch
and London
www.fishworks.co.uk

Serves: 2
Preparation time: 15 minutes
Cooking time: under 20 minutes

Ingredients:

A small glass of dry white wine
200g mussels in their shells
200g clams in their shells
75ml good olive oil
1 clove of garlic, chopped
6 raw prawns, peeled
6 langoustines, blanched and then peeled
100g monkfish fillet, sliced
2 scallops, sliced
3 tomatoes, skinned
Small handful of parsley
Pinch of sea salt
Enough cooked spaghetti for two
(let your appetite dictate, but I reckon on 75g per person)

Method:

1. Put the wine in a pan and bring to the boil, add the mussels and clams and cover. When they have all opened remove from the heat (discard any that have not opened) and leave to cool slightly. When cool enough to handle, remove the meat from the shells and reserve the cooking liquid.

2. In a large frying or roasting pan heat the olive oil gently, add the garlic and allow to colour. Add the peeled raw prawns, langoustines, scallops and monkfish and fry gently for 3-4 minutes.

3. Add the meat from the clams and mussels and then squeeze in the tomatoes so that some of the juice mixes into the oil. Add the parsley, a few tablespoons of the reserved cooking liquid and simmer for 2-3 minutes.

4. Add the spaghetti to the pan and toss it around to warm through quickly and serve.

Photography by Jason Lowe

Be part of the largest national dinner party... ever!

'My Favourite Night' dinner party

Struggling to come up with fun ideas on how to raise money for the BBC Children in Need Appeal? Look no further! As part of the appeal's 'Make it!' theme, 'This is my Favourite' has come up with a way to raise money and have fun with family and friends.

Over the course of the BBC Children in Need Appeal week we want restaurants from all over the country, catering colleges and hopefully you as well, to take part in what we hope will be the largest national dinner party... ever!

Here's how it works...

• First invite family and friends to a special 'My Favourite Night' dinner party on any evening between Saturday 11th November and Friday 17th November. Please ask your guests to make a cash donation that's equal to what they would have spent going out for a meal.

• Then go online to www.thisismyfavourite.co.uk to register your party.

• Once you've registered your party all you then have to do is decide on your 'My Favourite Night' dinner party menu. To help you decide we've put together our own suggested menu comprising an appetizer, a choice of meat and vegetarian main course and one pudding. The dishes aren't too complicated and cater for all tastes, and should guarantee that everything goes smoothly on the night!

• Alternatively you can choose from one of the other nine dinner party menus in the book or create your own, it's totally up to you. If you choose our suggested 'My Favourite Night' menu we've made it even easier for you by teaming up with Ocado, the online grocery delivery company in partnership with Waitrose. You can order a dinner party pack containing all the ingredients you need delivered on time, right to your door. Simply go to Ocado.com/dinnerparty for full details.

• You can even create your own special 'My Favourite Night' web page to send to your friends or order a pack of themed invitations from our website. There are lots of other goodies available online too, to help your dinner party go with a bang!

We hope you'll have a wonderful 'My Favourite Night' with your friends, join thousands of other diners in the largest national dinner party ever and raise lots of lovely money for the BBC Children in Need Appeal.

What could be easier? Simply register your party online at www.thisismyfavourite.co.uk

My Favourite Night ∎

Appetizer

Butternut Squash Soup

Ma

Chicken Breasts Stuffed with Rice and Mushroom

Make it!

'My Favourite Night' dinner party

Vegetarian Main
Mediterranean Vegetable Lasagne

Dessert
Vanilla Cheesecake

Appetizer: Butternut Squash Soup

Serves: 4
Preparation time: 20 minutes
Cooking time: 20 minutes

Ingredients:
4 tablespoons olive oil
2 butternut squash, peeled and finely diced
2 garlic cloves, peeled and chopped
2 leeks, sliced
1 litre vegetable stock
1/2 pint double cream
Handful of chives, chopped
Freshly ground black pepper

Method:
1. Sauté the diced butternut squash in a large pan with olive oil for approximately 5 minutes. Add the leeks and garlic and sauté for a further 2-3 minutes, stirring occasionally.
2. Season with salt and pepper and pour in vegetable stock. Bring this to the boil, then reduce the heat and simmer gently for 10-12 minutes, until the butternut squash is tender.
3. Stir in 5 tablespoons of double cream and heat for another minute or so.
4. Transfer the soup to a blender and blend until smooth.
5. Return to the pan and warm gently. Spoon into serving bowls and finish with a swirl of double cream, a sprinkling of chives and freshly ground black pepper - lovely!

Main: Chicken Breasts Stuffed with Rice and Mushrooms

Serves: 4
Preparation time: 30 minutes to 1 hour
Cooking time: 30 minutes to 1 hour

Ingredients:
Cocktail sticks
4 free range chicken breasts
80g wild and long grain rice
80g dry-cured bacon
30g dried wild mushrooms
4 red onions
2 sticks celery
2 cloves garlic
2 bunches parsley
20g butter
Balsamic vinegar
Rocket leaves
Salt and pepper
Olive oil

To Serve
Seasonal vegetables

Red Wine Sauce
55g shallots
150ml fruity red wine
150ml chicken stock
55g unsalted butter
1 tablespoon sweet soy sauce
1 tablespoon Worcestershire sauce
1 tablespoon olive oil
1 teaspoon sugar

Method:
Red Wine Sauce
1. Fry shallots in the olive oil and half the butter until tender, without browning.
2. Sprinkle in the sugar and stir. Cook for a further 1-2 minutes. Add the chicken stock and wine and boil hard until reduced by two thirds. Stir in the soy sauce and the Worcestershire sauce. Set aside.

Chicken
1. Pre-heat oven to the hottest setting.
2. Soak the mushrooms in 400ml of boiling water for 30 minutes then strain and rinse thoroughly.
3. Place rice into a large saucepan of water, bring to the boil and simmer for 15 minutes until tender.
4. Chop the garlic, red onions, parsley, celery and the dry-cured bacon. Fry the bacon until the fat is released. Add the garlic, red onions, celery and soaked mushrooms. Cook gently for a further 5 minutes. Add 2 teaspoons of the balsamic vinegar and reduce. Leave to cool.
5. Drain rice then stir in parsley and add to the bacon, garlic, red onions, celery and mushrooms. Season well and mix in the butter.

6. Slice the chicken breasts lengthways along the side to create a pouch, stopping $\frac{1}{2}$cm from the edge. Stuff the chicken with the rice mixture. Pin shut with cocktail sticks. Rest until the breasts firm up (about 20 minutes).
7. Using the olive oil fry the chicken skin, side down, in an ovenproof frying pan on a high heat. When the skin is lightly coloured turn over and place into the oven until cooked (about 10 minutes).
8. Dress the rocket leaves in a little balsamic vinegar. Rest the chicken breasts for 5 minutes before carving into 5 slices. Place on the bed of dressed rocket leaves.
9. Reheat the sauce. Cube the remaining butter. Whisk the sauce adding a few cubes of butter at a time and season. Drizzle the dish with red wine sauce.

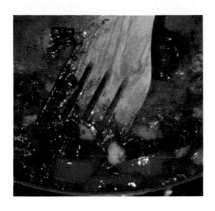

Vegetarian Main: Mediterranean Vegetable Lasagne served with a Rocket Salad

Serves: **4**
Preparation time: **15 minutes**
Cooking time: **30-40 minutes**

Ingredients:
Lasagne
2 cloves garlic, chopped
2 tablespoons olive oil
2 onions, cut into chunks
900g vegetables (aubergine, courgettes, red and yellow peppers, mushrooms)
400g tinned tomatoes, chopped
10g paprika
5g oregano
Salt and freshly ground black pepper
6 lasagne pasta sheets
125g cheddar cheese, grated

Rocket Salad
4 handfuls of rocket leaves
2 banana shallots
4 tomatoes
Balsamic vinegar
Freshly ground black pepper

Method:
Lasagne
1. Pre-heat oven to 190ºC, Gas Mark 5
2. Fry onions and vegetables in the olive oil for 10-12 minutes over a high heat, stirring continuously.
3. Add the tomatoes, paprika, oregano, garlic and bring to the boil. Season.
4. Place alternate layers of vegetables and pasta sheets in an oven proof dish, finishing with a layer of vegetables.
5. Top with cheese and bake for 25-30 minutes, until golden brown.

Rocket Salad
1. Wash rocket leaves and place 1 handful in individual side bowls. Chop shallots and tomatoes, place even amounts in each bowl. Dress with balsamic vinegar and a little freshly ground black pepper.

Dessert: Vanilla Cheesecake

This delicious cheesecake is best served with a selection of fresh fruit, we like raspberries.

Alternatively, try swapping the vanilla for the zest and juice of 2 lemons.

Serves: **8**
Preparation time: **15 minutes**

Ingredients:
12oz digestive biscuits, crushed
6oz soft butter or margarine
600g cream cheese
500g mascarpone
3 dessertspoons icing sugar
2 dessertspoons vanilla extract

Method:
1. Put crushed biscuits in a bowl with melted butter or margarine. When completely mixed, press into a spring based, loose-bottomed tin.
2. Put cream cheese and mascarpone in a large bowl and beat until smooth, then add icing sugar and vanilla and beat again. Transfer mixture into the tin.
3. Cover with cling film and put into the refrigerator for at least 2 hours.
4. Remove from the tin and decorate with fresh fruit.

My Favourite Night ■

Nick Vadis

In 2004, Nick came third in the country's most prestigious culinary competition, 'National Chef of the Year', achieving the highest position ever attained by a contract caterer in the competition. Nick has won many other culinary accolades in his career, including an array of gold medals on the national and international stage.

Sea Bass on Garlic Creamed Potatoes, Clam Vinaigrette and Parsley Nage

Chef Says

I like this dish for its simplicity and ease of service. The combination of creamed potatoes and bass work well together and the little acidity in the sauce complements the dish and adds a new dimension.

Eurest British Airways
Waterside
PO Box 365
Harmondsworth UB7 0GB
www.ba.com

Serves: **4**
Preparation time: **30 minutes**
Cooking time: **30 minutes**

Ingredients:
Sea Bass
4 fillets of sea bass

Garlic Mashed Potatoes
1kg russett potatoes
10 tablespoons double cream
3 tablespoons unsalted butter
10 cloves of garlic, peeled
Salt and pepper

Clam Vinaigrette
1kg palourde clams (very small)
1 small onion, finely diced
Garlic oil
1 celeriac, cooked and finely diced
2 tablespoons sun-dried tomato, finely diced
2 tablespoons fresh coriander
Lime juice
Salt and pepper

Parsley Nage
2 teaspoons shallots, minced
7 tablespoons dry white wine
7 tablespoons double cream
1 bunch flat leaf parsley
1 bunch spinach leaves
10 tablespoons chicken stock
Chopped garlic
1 tablespoon unsalted butter

Crab Beignets
75g trimmings from the sea bass flesh
50g white crab meat
1 egg white
Chives, chopped a pinch
20ml cream
Salt and pepper

Method:
Garlic Mashed Potatoes
1. Cut the potato into chunky pieces, bring to the boil, simmer then cook until soft.
2. Drain and place back into the pot and shake over the heat to evaporate excess water. Transfer to an electric mixer and mix or use a potato ricer.
3. Bring the cream and butter up to heat and add the riced potato. Check for seasoning and serve (should be light and luxurious).

Clam Vinaigrette
1. Wash the clams then place in a pan to cook until the shells open. Remove the meat from the shells and reserve. Also reserve the clam liquor from the pan.
2. Heat 1 tablespoon of olive oil in a pan, soften the onion and garlic without colour, place in a bowl then add the celeriac, tomatoes, clams and coriander.
3. Moisten with a little clam liquor and more olive oil. Season with lemon juice, salt and pepper, set aside.

Parsley Nage
1. Combine the shallots, garlic, wine and stock in a pan and cook until reduced by two thirds to about 4 tablespoons. Add the cream and return to the heat. Season and reserve. In a pan of boiling salted water add the parsley and spinach for about 10 seconds. Drain and refresh.
2. Squeeze out all the excess water and coarsely chop. Combine in a blender with the stock and cream reduction. Process until smooth.
3. Season and strain. Reserve the liquor and discard the solids. Check seasoning.

Sea Bass
1. Heat a little olive oil in a good sauté pan. When hot, season on both sides and place skin side down into it.
2. Cook for about 3 minutes and then carefully turn it over. Allow to cook on the flesh side and remove from the heat.

Crab Beignets
1. Place fish trimmings into a blender, add egg white and cream and blitz.
2. Fold in crab meat seasoning and chives, shape between spoons and deep fry until cooked.

© www.lisabarber.co.uk

108
Dinner Party Menu
Nick Wood

Appetizer: Asparagus Risotto

Main: Grilled Chicken and
Vegetable Salad

Dessert: Cheese Soufflé

Appetizer

Main

Dessert

Nick Wood

Nick is a man who has run with the best, having started out with an apprenticeship with Michel and Albert Roux at The Waterside Inn and Le Gavroche. He's since been private chef to some of the great epicurean households including Evelyn de Rothschild, Lord Weinstock, Valentino and The Royal Family. Nick's ethos is based on simplicity; great food can only come from great ingredients so source your produce very carefully. Nick insists the most important ingredients when cooking for friends are not caviar and truffles but charm, wit and effort! "Cooking for a dinner party is an act where the thrill begins before the first scene and continues well after the last curtain falls!"

Appetizer: Asparagus Risotto

Chef Says

I love this recipe as it takes me back to the Valentino days and Rome. It's uncomplicated in taste and texture... and a real no-brainer for the cook!

Top tip - keep it simple! Source your ingredients carefully and use the best (the best guide is Rick Stein's Food Heroes). Always stand up straight when cooking. It's most important to look after your back!!

www.nicholaswood.co.uk

Serves: 2
Preparation time: **35 minutes**
Cooking time: **35 minutes**

Ingredients:
100g arborio rice
¾ litre chicken stock
100g butter
200g asparagus, chopped into 1cm pieces
1 small onion, chopped
4 tablespoons parmesan, finely grated
Sea salt and pepper

Method:
1. Melt the butter in a saucepan. Add the onion and asparagus. Gently cook for 5 minutes to draw out some of the flavour.
2. Stir in the rice and cook for a minute before adding a little stock.
3. Start to add the stock a ladle at a time and wait until the liquid has evaporated before adding the next amount, stirring from time to time to make sure nothing sticks to the bottom of the pan. This process should take 20-22 minutes.
4. After 20 minutes the rice should take on a creamy texture and the stock should have been used up. Season and taste the rice to make sure it is cooked. Take off the heat for 1 minute, add a knob of butter and a tablespoon of parmesan and stir in. Serve the rice with extra grated parmesan cheese at the table.

Main: Grilled Chicken and Vegetable Salad

This is a recipe I used frequently whilst cooking down at the Cap d'Antibes where I would visit the market at 7.00am before the tourists made it unbearable! I would always buy my chickens from an ancient old lady who had held a stall on the market for more than 70 years! She had few chickens but they were excellent. The local seasonal vegetables were also excellent as was the strong scented basil and garlic. This recipe has travelled well with me all over and is a favourite in the warm summer months.

Serves: 2
Preparation time: 40 minutes
Cooking time: 20 minutes

Ingredients:

2 chicken breasts
1 aubergine
1 red pepper
1 green pepper
1 courgette
2 scallion onions
1 tomato
Handfuls of mixed leaf salad
1 clove of garlic, chopped
Small bunch of basil, chopped
Small bunch chives, chopped
10dl olive oil
5dl balsamic vinegar
2 tablespoons soy sauce
1 teaspoon honey
Salt and pepper

Method:

1. Marinate the chicken breasts for at least 2 hours in soy sauce, a tablespoon of olive oil, a tablespoon of vinegar, a tablespoon of mixed chives, basil, half the garlic, a teaspoon of honey, salt and pepper.
2. Chop the vegetables into 2 inch (or mouthsize) pieces, mix with olive oil and season.
3. Grill the vegetables separately and mix all together. Mix in the remaining chopped herbs and garlic. Place in a hot oven to heat for about 5 minutes before serving. Take out of the oven and leave to go warm (don't serve too hot as the heat will ruin the lettuce).
4. Grill the chicken breast for 3 minutes each side or until just cooked. It should be nice and dark. Take off the grill and leave on a board ready to slice.
5. Mix the lettuce leaves with the warm vegetables and serve on a plate or in an appropriate salad bowl. Slice the warm chicken and place on top.
6. Sprinkle a little balsamic vinegar and olive oil over the salad and serve whilst still warm.

Dessert: Cheese Soufflé

Not being a pudding fan I will always opt for cheese, but the ultimate way to finish a meal has to be a small cheese soufflé. You can always use your favourite cheese to supplement the Gruyère although a little Gruyère is always good as it gives the soufflé elasticity which holds it together well.

Serves: **2**
Preparation time: **25 minutes**
Cooking time: **10-12 minutes**

Ingredients:
3 fresh eggs
5ml milk
15g butter
15g plain flour
Nutmeg
50g Gruyère or other cheese of choice, grated
Seasoning

Method:
1. Pre-heat the oven to 200ºC. Butter 2 small soufflé dishes.
2. Melt the butter in a small saucepan and add the flour. Stir in and cook for 2 minutes then add the milk and keep stirring, creating a bechamel. Grate a little nutmeg and season.
3. Separate the eggs and whisk the egg yolks into the bechamel.
4. Whisk up the egg whites with a pinch of salt until firm.
5. Add half of the whites and half of the cheese to the bechamel and gently fold in. Fold in the remaining whites.
6. Spoon the mixture into the moulds leaving about 1cm free from the top of the mould. Place in a tray with 2cm of water in it, place onto the gas and bring to the boil. Place in the oven and cook for 7 minutes or until the soufflés have risen 1cm above the rim of the mould. Place some more cheese on top of the soufflé and cook for a further 3-4 minutes.
7. Take out of the oven and place immediately onto a small plate and serve.

Nora Sands

Nora is the loveable no-nonsense dinner lady who shot to fame in Jamie Oliver's TV series 'Jamie's School Dinners'. She was instrumental in helping him with his campaign to improve the nutritional value of food in Britain's schools. Nora's love of food dates back to her childhood days, digging up vegetables from her mum's vegetable patch to cook for the family's tea.

Oodles of Noodles

Chef Says

Be careful if you use chillies because the juices will stay on your fingers and will sting if you rub your eyes. Wash your hands with soap immediately after cutting or picking up chillies.

Nora Sands
Dinner Lady

Serves: **6**
Preparation time: **20 minutes**
Cooking time: **15 minutes**

Ingredients:

2 cloves of garlic, peeled and chopped as small as you can
Thumb-sized piece of fresh ginger, peeled and grated
1 fresh chilli, chopped and deseeded (optional)
1 courgette, sliced into strips
1 red pepper, deseeded and sliced into thin strips
1 carrot, peeled first, then peeled into strips using the vegetable peeler.
125g mushrooms, sliced
5 spring onions, sliced
125g mange tout
4 tablespoons sesame oil
1 teaspoon curry paste or powder
115g beansprouts
300g fresh cooked egg noodles or 250g dried
3 tablespoons water
15g pack fresh coriander, chopped
2 tablespoons soy sauce

Method:

1. Prepare the garlic, ginger, chilli, courgette, pepper, carrot, mushrooms, spring onions and mange tout. Weigh out the other ingredients.
2. Remember to chop the vegetables to the size given in the ingredients list to make sure that everything cooks evenly and is ready at the same time.
3. Heat the wok or frying pan and add the sesame oil. When the oil is very hot add the garlic, ginger and chilli (if you are using it) and stir with a wooden spatula for a few seconds. Add the rest of the prepared vegetables and curry paste or powder. Keep on a high heat and fry, stirring all the time.
4. After a few minutes add the beansprouts and noodles.
5. While stirring, add the water, coriander and soy sauce. Stir well for a couple more minutes. The stir-fry is ready when the mushrooms and peppers have just wilted or shrivelled.

Taken from 'Nora's Dinners'. Published by Collins, priced £12.99.

Photography by Véronique Leplat

Ollie Luscombe

After travelling the world, 'the local boy' came back to Holbeton in Devon. Being able to use fantastic local produce and combining them with styles he learned along the way, Ollie hopes to produce good tasty food.

Best End of Lamb with a Parsley Crust and a Rosemary and Parmesan Polenta

Chef Says

I like this dish because it's clean and simple. The lamb coupled with the polenta is fantastic in Spring; the colours reflect the season.

The Dartmoor Union Inn
Fore Street
Holbeton
Devon PL8 1NE
Telephone: 01752 830288
www.dartmoorunion.co.uk

Serves: 4
Preparation time: 20-30 minutes
Cooking time: 15-20 minutes

Ingredients:
Herb Crusted Lamb
4 x 150g best end of lamb
(you can ask your butcher to trim skin and French trim)

Parsley Crust
25g parsley, chopped
50g butter
50g fresh white breadcrumbs
1 large clove of garlic

Rosemary and Parmesan Polenta
1½ pints of milk
25g butter
150g polenta
25g rosemary, chopped
1 large clove of garlic, crushed
50g parmesan, freshly grated

Method:
Herb Crust
(Best to prepare 24 hours before)
1. Soften the butter and blend together with the breadcrumbs, garlic and parsley.
2. Add a pinch of salt and pepper.
3. Place the mixture between 2 sheets of greaseproof paper and roll out flat (approximately 3mm thick) then leave in the fridge to firm up.
4. Once chilled, cut into squares (similar size to the portions of lamb).

Herb Crusted Lamb
1. Season then sear the lamb in a hot frying pan for 1 minute on either side so all the meat is sealed.
2. Place a pre-cut square of the herb crust on top of the lamb (removing the greaseproof paper) and roast in the oven for 10 minutes at 180°C.
3. Once cooked, leave to rest for 5 minutes then cut into 3 cutlets and serve on top of the rosemary and parmesan polenta.

Rosemary and Parmesan Polenta
1. Bring the milk to the boil with the butter, rosemary and garlic.
2. Once boiled, slowly stir in the polenta and cook out for approximately 5 minutes until thick (it should be the same consistency as porridge).
3. Add the parmesan and beat with a wooden spoon until smooth, then serve.

Paul Askew

The London Carriage Works is a recipient of a Harden's Rémy for the 'Top Ten Regional Restaurants' and is located on the ground floor of the multi-award winning Hope Street Hotel.

Mr Renucci's Panettone Bread and Butter Pudding

Serves: 4
Preparation time: 30 minutes
Cooking time: 40 minutes

Ingredients:

100g butter
1 panettone, sliced thickly and buttered
450ml milk, full fat
100g vanilla sugar
4 large eggs
Nutmeg to taste, freshly grated

Method:

1. Rub the butter liberally over the inside of an ovenproof dish. Thickly cut and butter the panettone and lay overlapping in the dish. Sprinkle with a little sugar and nutmeg. Repeat this to achieve at least 2 layers deep.

Egg Custard

1. Warm the milk in a saucepan. Lightly mix together the sugar and eggs in a basin and then pour on the hot milk. Strain through a conical sieve onto the panettone, sprinkling extra sugar and nutmeg onto the top layer. Leave to rest for 1 hour. Bake in a pre-heated oven 180°C or Gas Mark 4 for 30-40 minutes until it soufflés.
2. Serve hot with a toffee or butterscotch sauce and seasonal berries.

Chef Says

This dish is one of my comfort food favourites, inspired by an old Italian friend who produced panettone at every possible opportunity. It is delicious.

Top tip - to make vanilla sugar, half fill an air-tight container with granulated sugar. Add a split vanilla bean and cover with the rest of the sugar. Store for a couple of weeks shaking occasionally. This will infuse the sugar with the vanilla flavour and is a fantastic ingredient for puddings.

The London Carriage Works
40 Hope Street
Liverpool L1 9DA
Telephone: 0151 705 2222
www.tlcw.co.uk

Paul Fielding

Paul started his career at the Grand Hotel in Birmingham and progressed to become Head Chef at Aston Villa Football Club. He has also worked and travelled extensively throughout Europe and is in the process of writing a book about his career and life. In his spare time, Paul says he likes to unwind and play a round or two of golf, although his latest achievement has been to complete the Flora London Marathon 2006.

Herb and Pepper Crusted Salmon served with a Mussel Broth and Ginger Noodles

Chef Says

This is a firm favourite of mine, bringing together a superb mix of Scottish salmon and mussels. The ingredients combine perfectly and are great for a romantic summer dinner.

The Macdonald Bush Hotel
The Borough
Farnham
Surrey GU9 7NN
Telephone: 0870 400 8225
www.bushhotel.co.uk

Serves: 4
Preparation time: 30 minutes
Cooking time: 15 minutes

Ingredients:
800g salmon (Scottish)
20g cracked black pepper
20g herbs (dill, parsley, chives), chopped
400g fresh loch mussels
180ml double cream
1 cup dry white wine
2 tomatoes
Small bunch of chives
50g fresh stem ginger
1 shallot
1 clove of garlic
1 lemon, juiced
1 packet of egg noodles
100g butter (unsalted)
Salt and pepper
1 cup sunflower oil
Leeks for garnish

Method:
1. Ask your fishmonger to cut the salmon for you into 200g fillets.
2. Place the noodles in warm water to soften.
3. Mix the chopped herbs and cracked black pepper together and place on a rolled out piece of cling film on a flat surface. Place the salmon, meat side down, on the herb and pepper crust, pressing slightly. The crust will stick to the salmon and this can be placed in the fridge for half an hour to let the flavours infuse.
4. Peel and grate the ginger and place in a pot with a little water. Boil until it reduces and the ginger becomes a slightly thick consistency.
5. Using a non-stick pan, place a spoon of oil and allow it to heat slightly until smoking. Place the salmon fillets in face down for 2-3 minutes. Turn the salmon and repeat the process on the other side. Remove from the pan and place in a non-stick oven dish. Finish in the oven at 180°C for 7 minutes.
6. While this is cooking add the wine to the salmon pan with the chopped shallot and crushed garlic, followed by the mussels. Cover the pan for a few moments. When the mussels have opened, remove them and add the cream to the wine reduction.
7. Keeping a few mussels in the shell for garnish, remove all other mussel meat and add to the wine and cream reduction with a squeeze of lemon juice. When the sauce starts to thicken add in the diced tomato and chives. Set sauce aside keeping it warm.
8. Using a non-stick frying pan, place a tablespoon of oil and a knob of butter with a little of the reduced ginger. Sauté lightly for a few minutes and then add your pre-softened noodles and toss until they are warmed through.
9. Place the noodles in the centre of the plate and, using a tablespoon, spoon a little of the mussel broth around the noodles. Remove the salmon and place herb side up on top of the noodles. Some finely chopped leek, deep fried, makes a nice garnish along with a couple of cooked mussels still in their shells.

MACDONALD
BUSH HOTEL

Paul Montgomery

Paul returned to his roots in rural Northumberland to take over the role of Executive Head Chef at De Vere Slaley Hall after a spell aboard a luxury yacht in the Mediterranean rustling up dishes for Madonna, Sophia Loren and Anthony Hopkins. He returned to his native North East after missing the hustle and bustle of a large kitchen and is in charge of cuisine for thousands of guests, including world-famous golfers and the England football squad, who train at the hotel when they are in the region.

Dark Chocolate Bavarois with Fresh Honeycomb

Chef Says

Pudding lovers indulge with this soft and velvety bavarois enveloped in crisp cool chocolate. For a real dinner party wow factor, serve with fresh honeycomb - a favourite ingredient of mine which is now readily available in supermarkets.

Top tip - the secret to the perfect bavarois lies in heating the milk custard for the correct length of time. A great way to test whether the milk has thickened sufficiently is to press your fingertip onto the back of a spoon that has been dipped into the custard. If the mixture stays in place and does not drip down into the impression left, then the mixture is ready.

De Vere Slaley Hall
Hexham
Northumberland NE47 0BX
Telephone: 01434 673350
www.devere.co.uk

Serves: 4-6
Preparation time: 5 minutes
Cooking time: 90 minutes including setting time

Ingredients:

Bavarois
225ml milk
55g (approx 1 large) egg yolk
14g gelatine (approx 3 sheets), soaked in water according to packet instructions
50g caster sugar
225g double or whipping cream
55g dark chocolate, melted
Fresh bee's honeycomb, cut into cubes

Chocolate Sauce
285ml milk
40g caster sugar
7g unsalted butter
14g cornflour
14g cocoa

Chocolate Edging and Ruffle
200g dark chocolate

Method:

Bavarois
1. Cream the egg yolk with the sugar.
2. Boil the milk and whisk into the sugar cream. Replace on a low heat and stir until the mixture thickens into a custard.
3. Blend in the melted chocolate.
4. Remove from the heat and stir in the soaked gelatine. Continue to stir gently until the gelatine has dissolved.
5. Strain the mixture (a tea strainer works really well for this) and cool until it is almost setting (about 20-30 minutes).

6. Half whip the cream and fold into the custard until clear. Pour the mixture into individual non-stick moulds, preferably round in shape, and chill.
7. Remove from the mould, once set, by gently shaking onto a plate and position a piece of honeycomb alongside.
8. Wrap in chocolate and add a decorative chocolate ruffle to the top (see method below).
9. Spot the chocolate sauce onto the plate (see method below).

Chocolate Sauce
1. Mix the cornflour in a bowl with a little of the milk and the cocoa.
2. Boil the remaining milk and strain.
3. Stir in the cornflour mixture.
4. Return to a clean saucepan and gently bring to the boil.
5. Mix in the sugar and butter.
6. Sieve and chill before serving.

Chocolate Edging and Ruffle
1. Melt the chocolate until smooth and runny.
2. Spread evenly over a stainless steel tray and freeze for 15-20 minutes.
3. Remove and return to room temperature.
4. Using a scraper, scrape a long thin strip of chocolate to wrap around the bavarois.
5. For ruffle decoration repeat the method above and pleat the chocolate by curling the strip, keeping the bottom nipped together.

Paul and Jeanne Rankin

As well as appearing on a number of TV shows, Paul Rankin runs a successful restaurant and café business in his native Ireland with his wife and fellow chef, Jeanne. Paul and Jeanne have appeared together in three series of a television culinary journey called 'Gourmet Ireland' and have also written five books. Paul hosted three series of 'The Rankin Challenge', and has appeared on 'Masterchef', 'Saturday Kitchen' and ' The Good Food Show' although he is most noted as a favourite on 'Ready Steady Cook'.

Sticky Toffee Pudding with a Bushmills Butterscotch Sauce

Chef Says

An all-time favourite, this sticky toffee pudding gets real depth of flavour from the intense sweetness of the dates. The generous dose of Bushmills Irish whiskey cuts through the butterscotch sauce with great character.

www.rankingroup.co.uk

Serves: 6-8
Preparation time: **10 minutes**
Cooking time: **35 minutes**

Ingredients:
Sticky Toffee Pudding
200g fresh dates, stoned and finely chopped
175g self-raising flour
1 teaspoon bicarbonate of soda
1 teaspoon vanilla essence
1 teaspoon coffee essence
100ml milk
85g unsalted butter
140g sugar
2 eggs, beaten just to break the yolks
Vegetable oil, for greasing
Whipped cream, to serve

Butterscotch Sauce
3 tablespoons unsalted butter
8 tablespoons light golden brown sugar
200ml whipping cream
200ml Bushmills Irish whiskey
1 tablespoon vanilla essence

Method:
1. Preheat the oven to 180ºC, 350ºF, Gas Mark 4.
2. Pour 175ml of boiling water over the dates and set aside to soak and cool. Sift the flour and soda together.
3. Add the essences to the milk.
4. Cream the butter and sugar together until light and fluffy. Add the eggs slowly, waiting until it has been incorporated each time, before adding more.
5. Fold the flour and milk alternately into the egg mixture. Lastly, pour in the dates. The mix will be rather light and runnier than a cake batter. Ladle into 6-8 greased individual moulds and place on a baking sheet in the centre of the oven. Bake for 30 minutes approximately, until the puddings are firm and starting to pull away from the sides of the moulds.
6. Remove from the oven and turn out onto a wire rack to cool.
7. To make the butterscotch sauce, put the butter in a medium-sized saucepan, over medium-high heat. When the butter is bubbling, add the brown sugar. Stir together for about 3 minutes, until the sugar has dissolved, and the whole mass is foaming and bubbling. Carefully pour in the cream, followed by the Bushmills, and turn down the heat. Let it all come together and boil for about another minute or two, and then remove from the heat. Add the vanilla. Allow to cool slightly.
8. To serve, place the puddings on warm plates and ladle a generous spoonful of the sauce over each one. Dollops of whipped cream will top them off perfectly. If wrapped in cling film, the puddings keep well for a couple of days, and can be reheated in just a minute or two in the microwave or covered in some of the sauce in a medium oven.

Taken from 'New Irish Cookery' by Paul and Jeanne Rankin. Published by BBC Books.

Portrait Photography by Khara Pringle.

Photography by Gareth Morgans © BBC Worldwide

Philip Burgess

When Philip was 16 years old, his passion for cooking led him to take a job at his local pub - The Dartmoor Inn at Lydford!
After working at top restaurants in France and London and running the kitchen at The Arundell Arms at Lifton for 25 years,
Philip eventually returned to buy The Dartmoor Inn. Together with his wife Karen, they have turned a 'run-down boozer'
into one of the leading pub-restaurants in the country.

Casserole of Sea Fishes with Saffron and Leeks

Chef Says

This dish is a clear favourite of mine that
has been tried and tested over the years.
I like it because it can be changed to
incorporate different fish and uses
whatever is available at the time.

Dartmoor Inn
Moorside
Lydford
Okehampton
Devon EX20 4AY
Telephone: 01822 820221

Serves: 4
Preparation time: 30 minutes
Cooking time: 10-15 minutes

Ingredients:

2 whole dover or lemon sole, filleted
8 scallops, trimmed
225g monkfish, trimmed
225g red mullet fillets
1 leek, cut finely in cross section diameter
2 tablespoons white wine
$\frac{1}{2}$ pint fish stock, reduced
2 bay leaves
Salt and pepper
$\frac{1}{2}$ pint cream
Good pinch of saffron
75g unsalted butter, cubed

Method:

1. Prepare all the fish and cut into
   2 inch strips, season and arrange in
   a heavy-bottomed pan with the
   scallops, fish stock, wine, leek, bay
   leaves and saffron.
2. Bring gently to the boil on top of the
   stove, cover with butter papers and
   place in a fairly hot oven. Cook for
   8-10 minutes.
3. Remove the fish from the pan and
   arrange on serving plates. Keep warm.
4. Strain the cooking liquors and reduce
   by two thirds, add the cream and bring
   to the boil. Simmer for 2 minutes, whisk
   in the butter and ensure the seasoning
   is correct.
5. Pour over the fish and serve
   immediately with rice or boiled
   potatoes and green vegetables.

Rainer Becker

ZUMA, since its opening in May 2002, continues to bring compelling food, immaculate service and glamorous design to London's Knightsbridge. At both ZUMA and ROKA - which opened on London's Charlotte Street to equally huge acclaim in 2004 - Rainer offers his customers a sophisticated and contemporary take on the traditional Japanese 'Izakaya' style of informal eating and drinking. 2007 sees Rainer and Arjun bring ZUMA to an even wider audience with the opening of ZUMA, Hong Kong.

Barley Miso Marinated Chicken

Chef Says

Choose organic corn fed chicken if possible. This is a great summer dish, with lots of flavour and it's quick and easy to prepare. Perfect if you don't want to spend too much time in the kitchen cooking.

Top tip - soak the garlic in water to make peeling easier.

Zuma Restaurant
5 Raphael Street
Knightsbridge SW7 1DL
Telephone: 020 7584 1010
www.zumarestaurant.com

Serves: 2
Preparation time: 20 minutes
(after marinating for 24 hours)
Cooking time: 15 minutes

Ingredients:

2 baby chickens - boned spatchcock style
2 cedar wood squares

Marinade
120ml vegetable oil
4 cloves garlic, finely chopped
60ml ginger juice
3g sichimi pepper
160ml barley miso
40ml soy
60ml sake
40ml mirin
12 shallots, finely chopped

Method:

1. Heat the mirin and sake to burn off the alcohol and allow to cool.
2. Bone the baby chickens.
3. Mix all the marinade ingredients together. Reserve a quarter of the marinade to use as topping later.
4. Marinate the chicken in the remaining marinade for 24 hours.
5. After 24 hours remove the chickens from the marinade. Grill to get a bar mark.
6. Place on the cedar wood square, cover with the reserved marinade and roast in the oven for 12-14 minutes.
7. Serve.

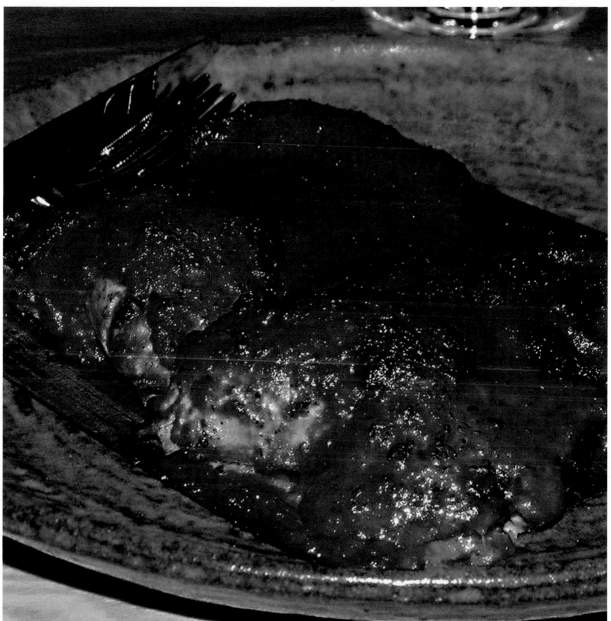

128
Raj and Mukesh Joshi

Raj and Mukesh Joshi first got involved in the food business when they started working in their dad's vegetarian restaurant in 1977. As time progressed, they learned the art of how to make a great curry and this is reflected in the awards they have received such as 'Best Balti' award and the 'Overall Winner' trophy at the Nightlife Awards 2002.

Vegetable Biryani with Dahi Wada

Chef Says

Vegetable biryani is a delicious 'meal-in-one' dish with both rice and curry. It's also very filling so don't be tempted to over-fill your plate!

Jyoti
569-571 Stratford Road
Sparkhill
Birmingham B11 4LS
Telephone: 0121 766 7199

Serves: **4**
Biryani preparation time: **30 minutes**
Biryani cooking time: **30 minutes**

Dahi Wada preparation time: **5 hours**
Dahi Wada cooking time: **10 minutes, plus 3 hours soaking in yoghurt**

Ingredients:
2 cups basmati rice
1 cup steamed vegetables (green peas, beans, cauliflower, carrots etc.)
2 medium onions, chopped
2 tablespoons raisins
2 tablespoons cashew nuts or slivered almonds
2 teaspoons salt
1 teaspoon turmeric powder
½ teaspoon cinnamon powder
¼ teaspoon each clove powder, nutmeg powder, chilli powder, coriander powder
3 tablespoons butter

Dahi Wada
1 cup coarse matpe (bean flour)
1 litre yoghurt
1 tablespoon cumin powder
2 green chillies
1 stem curry leaves
250ml oil
Salt to taste

Method:
1. Pre-heat oven to 375ºF, Gas Mark 5.
2. Soak the basmati rice in water for 30 minutes. Rinse and drain well.
3. Melt half the butter in a frying pan and sauté the onions, cashew nuts and raisins until golden brown. Keep aside.
4. Melt the rest of the butter in the pan and add the rice. Fry until it is coated in butter and not sticking together.
5. Add all the spices and mix well. Empty the rice into a baking pan, add salt and 1½ cups of water.
6. Place in the oven and cook for 20 minutes or until the rice is cooked.
7. Add the vegetables, onions, raisins and cashew nuts to the rice and mix well. Serve.

Dahi Wada
1. To make the dumplings soak the flour for 5 hours in water (enough to cover).
2. Swill and mix the resulting paste together until thick and soft.
3. Add salt, then form dumpling shapes with hands - aim for golf ball size.
4. Place in the palm of the hand, pat until round and make a hole in the centre. Deep fry in the oil until light brown.
5. Allow to cool. Soak the dumplings in the yoghurt for 3 hours. Chop green chillies finely and sprinkle over the dumplings with the cumin powder, salt and curry leaves. Serve.

130
Dinner Party Menu
Raymond Blanc

Appetizer: Gruyère, Ham and Mushroom Salad with Cream and Mustard Dressing

Main: Pot-au-feu of Braised Pork Belly

Dessert: Cherry Clafoutis

Appetizer

Main

Dessert

Raymond Blanc

Born in Besançon, France in 1949, Raymond Blanc is acknowledged as one of the finest chefs in the world. His exquisite cooking has received tributes from every national and international guide to culinary excellence.

Appetizer: Gruyère, Ham and Mushroom Salad with Cream and Mustard Dressing

Chef Says

I wish I could sit down with you for this meal as I have shared it so many times with my parents in my native Franche-Comté. This simple, wholesome menu demonstrates the appeal of French cuisine.

Raymond Blanc
Chef Patron
Le Manoir aux Quat'Saisons
Church Road
Great Milton OX44 7PD
Telephone: 01844 278881
www.manoir.com

A simple, every day salad from my native county, Franche-Comté. Most of my English friends speed past it on their way from Paris to the south of France and in doing so bypass one of the loveliest and most hospitable areas of the country. It produces some of the very best cream and cheeses in France, which are used extensively in its cuisine.

Serves: **4**
Preparation time: **20 minutes**

Ingredients:
Salad
300g smoked ham or jambon de Paris
100g Gruyère cheese
200g firm, fresh button mushrooms
2 chicory heads
100g frisée lettuce
100g lamb's lettuce
1 tablespoon fresh chives, chopped

Dressing
1 small tablespoon Dijon mustard
5 tablespoons whipping cream
1 tablespoon white wine vinegar
5 tablespoons grape seed oil or extra virgin olive oil
Sea salt and freshly ground black pepper

Method:
1. To prepare the salad ingredients, cut the ham and cheese into strips. Cut the mushrooms into slices 3mm thick. Cut the base off the chicory and remove any damaged outer leaves. Cut each chicory head in half lengthways and slice into 2cm chunks.
2. To make the dressing, put the mustard in a small bowl and whisk in the cream, then the white wine vinegar. Gradually whisk in the oil and then season to taste with 2 pinches of sea salt and 2 pinches of black pepper.
3. To finish the salad, put the chicory, lettuce, ham, cheese and mushrooms in a large bowl and mix with the dressing. Scatter the chopped chives on top and serve.

Main: Pot-au-feu of Braised Pork Belly

Pot-au-feu is a French peasant dish where the meat, vegetables and broth are all cooked together in one pot. It is often made with a plump and tasty chicken rather than pork. In 1664 King Henri IV of France, a good and great PR man, decreed that every peasant should have a poule au pot, or 'chicken in a pot', on Sundays. I suppose if the kings that followed him had shared his wisdom and empathy, France might still have a monarchy today...

Serves: **4**
Preparation time: **30 minutes**
Cooking time: **3 hours**

Ingredients:

1.5kg organic or free range belly of pork, boned and skin removed (leaving a small layer of fat)
3 fresh sage leaves
3 litres water
4 carrots, peeled
6 garlic cloves, peeled
1 bouquet garni (made with 2 bay leaves, 6 thyme sprigs, 2 sage leaves, 1 rosemary sprig and 1 marjoram sprig, tied together)
2 celery sticks, cut into 7.5cm lengths and tied together in a bundle
4 banana shallots or ordinary shallots, peeled but left whole
2 leeks, 2 outer layers removed, cut into 7.5cm lengths and tied together in a bundle
$^1/_2$ savoy cabbage, cut in 4, with the core left in to hold the leaves together
4 medium potatoes, such as Desirée, peeled and cut into quarters
A handful of fresh flat-leaf parsley, roughly chopped
Sea salt and freshly ground black pepper

Method:

1. To prepare the pork, place the belly of pork fat-side down and season the flesh with 3 pinches of salt and a pinch of pepper. Lay the sage leaves in a line along the centre, then take the thickest part of the belly and roll it up as tightly as possible. Tie a piece of string tightly around the rolled belly. Repeat this 5 or 6 times so the meat holds its shape during cooking. In order to hold the belly tightly and tie it at the same time, it is easier to have a friend helping you.

2. Brown the pork, on a medium heat in a large non-stick frying pan, without oil or butter for 12–15 minutes, until golden brown all over.

3. To braise the pork, place the pork belly into a large casserole dish. Pour in the cold water, add 1 tablespoon of salt and bring to the boil over a high heat. With a ladle, skim off any impurities that rise to the surface. Lower the heat and cook on a gentle simmer (with bubbles just breaking the surface) for 1 hour. Fast cooking would make the meat very tough.

4. To cook the vegetables, add the carrots, garlic and bouquet garni and cook for a further 30 minutes. Then add all the remaining ingredients except the parsley and cook for 1 hour longer, until the meat and vegetables are tender. Stir in the parsley, adjust the seasoning and serve directly from the pot to the table. Carve the pork in front of your guests or, if you are shy, in the privacy of your kitchen.

Dessert: Cherry Clafoutis

Clafoutis is a great family dish. Of course, my mum's recipe was the best, and it is now one of our bestsellers at the Le Petit Blanc brasseries. Everyone should know how to make this dessert. It is so easy to prepare and your children, husband, wife and friends will love you two thousand times more for it!

Put the clafoutis in the oven just before you sit down to eat your meal, then it will be at the right temperature when you serve it; just warm is best.

Serves: **4**
Preparation time: **30 minutes,
plus 2 hours' marinating**
Cooking time: **30-35 minutes**

Ingredients:

Cherries
500g fresh cherries, stoned
**2 tablespoons caster sugar,
plus extra to serve**
2 tablespoons Kirsch (optional)

Dish
10g unsalted butter, melted
3 tablespoons caster sugar

Batter
100g plain white flour
A pinch of salt
3 organic or free range eggs
1 organic or free range egg yolk
6 tablespoons caster sugar
Zest of 1 lemon, finely grated
**6 drops of natural vanilla extract
(optional)**
150ml milk
150ml whipping cream
75g unsalted butter

Method:

Marinating the Cherries

1. Mix the cherries with the sugar and the kirsch, if using, and leave for 2 hours to maximise their flavour.

Preparing the Baking Dish

1. Brush the inside of a round or oval cast iron or china baking dish, 20cm (8 inch) in diameter and 5cm (2 inch) deep, with the melted butter.
2. Sprinkle in the caster sugar and shake the dish so it coats the inside evenly. This will give the clafoutis a lovely crust during cooking. Pre-heat the oven to 180ºC, 350ºF, Gas Mark 4.

Making the Batter

1. Put the flour and salt in a mixing bowl and make a well in the centre. Add the eggs, egg yolk, sugar, lemon zest and the vanilla, if using. With a whisk, slowly incorporate the egg mixture into the flour until smooth. Whisk in the milk and cream.
2. In a small saucepan, heat the butter until it turns a pale hazelnut colour, then whisk it into the batter while still hot.

Finishing the Clafoutis

1. Mix the cherries and their juices into the batter and then pour into the baking dish. Bake for 30-35 minutes, until the blade of a knife inserted into the mixture comes out completely clean. Sprinkle a little caster sugar over and serve warm.

Régis Crepy

Régis and his wife, Martine, have created their very own 'little pocket of France' at the delightful 15th century Great House, set in the heart of the historic market town of Lavenham in Suffolk. The award winning Great House is the perfect start for a relaxing stay, either 'en famille', with your best friends, as a romantic get-away or just as a delightful place to eat. Régis also owns Maison Bleue in Bury St Edmunds and Il Punto in Ipswich.

Lime and Mascarpone Crunch

Chef Says

A melt in the mouth refreshing summer dessert.

Top tip - make sure the slices of pineapple are very tender once cooked in the sugar so that they melt in your mouth.

The Great House
Market Place
Lavenham
Sudbury
Suffolk CO10 9QZ
Telephone: 01787 247431
www.greathouse.co.uk

Serves: 4
Preparation time: 30 minutes

Ingredients:
1 pack of ready-made puff pastry
1 fresh pineapple

Coco Mousse
400g coconut purée
400g coconut, grated
400g cream
120g sugar
4 gelatine leaves

Crème Anglaise with Lime & Mascarpone
500g mascarpone
400g cream
200g sugar
120g egg yolk
5 lime zests
200g lime juice
5g gelatine leaves

Method:
'Arlette' Puff Pastry
1. Brush the pastry with water. Roll it into a log and seal with water. Wrap and refrigerate until very cold.
2. Slice the log into thin slices.
3. With a rolling pin, roll over icing sugar until very thin. Then use a cookie cutter to make it into a perfect circle.
4. Place on a baking tray with greaseproof paper. Dust the 'Arlettes' with more icing sugar.
5. Bake at 180ºC until golden. Allow to cool.

Confit of Pineapple
1. Slice the pineapple.
2. Cook the pineapple slices in sugar syrup.
3. Once cold, cut into neat triangles and put to one side.

Coco Mousse
1. Put the gelatine leaves in a little cold water.
2. Mix the coconut purée and grated coconut together.
3. Whip the cream and sugar to a soft peak.
4. Melt the gelatine leaves in the water and mix it with the coconut mix, adding the whipped cream delicately. Put aside.

Crème Anglaise with Lime & Mascarpone
1. Melt the gelatine leaves in a little cold water.
2. Boil the sugar and then add the egg yolks and cook at 87ºC.
3. Beat it in the mixer while hot, adding the zest of limes and lime juice and also the gelatine melted reserve.

To Finish:
1. Beat the mascarpone in the mixer and slowly incorporate the crème anglaise with the lime. Build the dessert in the following order - coco mousse, arlette, crème anglaise, confit of pineapple, spun sugar (optional).

Rick Stein

Besides having written eleven popular cookbooks, Rick Stein has made eight BBC TV cooking series which have gone down very well internationally, particularly in Australia and New Zealand. Rick's passion is still for seafood; as he says, "nothing is more exhilarating than fresh fish simply cooked". The daily bounty of perfectly fresh fish brought in by the local fishermen has contributed to the success of Rick's Seafood Restaurant in Padstow, Cornwall.

Salmon Marinated with Dill and Pernod

Chef Says

I probably enjoy salmon raw or lightly cooked in citrus juice more than any other way. The aniseed taste of the Pernod complements the flavour of the dill beautifully. You could also use anisette, a slightly sweet aniseed-flavoured liqueur, but if using this, leave out the sugar.

The Seafood Restaurant
Riverside
Padstow
Cornwall PL28 8BY
Telephone: 01841 532700
www.rickstein.com

Serves: 4
Preparation time: 15 minutes
Cooking time: 5 minutes to rest

Ingredients:
400g piece of unskinned salmon fillet
85ml sunflower oil
Juice of 1/2 lemon
1 tablespoon dill, chopped
2 teaspoons Pernod
1 teaspoon caster sugar
1 teaspoon chives, chopped
1/2 teaspoon salt and 10 turns of the black pepper mill

Method:
1. Put 4 plates into the fridge together with the salmon fillet and leave them to get really cold. Shortly before serving, mix all the remaining ingredients together in a bowl.
2. Put the salmon fillet skin-side down on a board. Hold a long, thin-bladed knife at a 45° angle and, starting at the tail end of the fillet, cut the salmon into very thin slices. Lay the slices, slightly overlapping, on each chilled plate and spoon over the dressing. Leave for 5 minutes before serving.

Taken from Rick Stein's Food Heroes Another Helping - BBC Books.

Ross Burden

It is well documented that Ross' successful television career began after reaching the final of 'MasterChef 1993'. Ross loves teaching and demonstrating the art of cooking and regularly appears at internationally renowned cookery schools. Recently, Ross prepared over 2000 canapés for the VIP guests at the Friends of the Earth benefit concert and was a runaway success on 'Celebrity X Factor, Battle of the Stars' as part of Simon Cowell's group 'The Chefs'. Ross makes no excuses, as he says himself; "We were dreadful!"

Flourless Chocolate Torte with Raspberries

Chef Says

This is a great comfort food any time of the year and it is so easy to make. Eat it warm or cold, winter or summer; you will enjoy this one.

Top tip - the more gently you fold in the egg whites the softer the torte will be, but don't worry if it doesn't look perfect when you take it out of the oven, it will taste fantastic.

www.rossburden.com

Serves: 8
Preparation time: **25 minutes**
Cooking time: **25 minutes**

Ingredients:
300g chocolate (minimum 70% cocoa solids)
200g butter
4 eggs
200g caster sugar

To Garnish
Crème fraiche
300g raspberries, fresh or frozen
50g caster sugar

Method:
1. Melt 100g of the chocolate over water and pour over a robust tray, e.g. the back of a clean roasting tray and allow to cool.
2. Add the rest of the chocolate and the butter into the same bowl and allow to melt and mix. Stir well.
3. Separate the eggs and beat 100g of sugar into each bowl, making the whites into soft peaks. Beat the yolk mixture into the chocolate and butter mixture, beat in half of the whites and then fold the rest of the whites into the mixture.
4. Grease and dust with cocoa, a 20cm cake tin. A greased paper disc underneath is a great idea. Bake at 160°C for about 25 minutes; the centre should just wobble. Allow it to cool and turn out upside down. If it has souffléd, press gently.
5. Serve warm with raspberries warmed with the sugar until it's dissolved, and the crème fraiche. Use the 100g of cooled chocolate broken into chards for decoration or to crumble over the top.

© Photography by Dan Jones

Russell Brown

Sienna was opened in April 2003 by Russell and Eléna Brown, and since then has gained a reputation for fine food and wine. Their philosophy revolves around using good seasonal produce, making everything possible in-house and running an interesting and diverse wine list whilst providing a friendly service in a relaxed and stylish environment. The restaurant was awarded 2 AA Rosettes in November 2003 and is Michelin and Good Food Guide listed.

Asparagus Benedict

Chef Says

English asparagus is one highlight of the culinary calendar, and to heighten the enjoyment we only use asparagus during this short period in May and June. This recipe is elegant comfort food at its best!

Top tip - poach the eggs in a deep pan of simmering water with 1 tablespoon white wine vinegar. Refresh in iced water and warm through in simmering water to serve. They can be held in the fridge for an hour or so before service.

Sienna Restaurant
36 High West Street
Dorchester
Dorset DT1 1UP
Telephone: 01305 250022
www.siennarestaurant.co.uk

Serves: 4 as a starter
Preparation time: 30 minutes
Cooking time: 10 minutes

Ingredients:
2 English muffins, split in half
4 large organic eggs
4 slices Denhay ham
or other air-dried ham
16 medium asparagus spears
1 egg yolk
200g unsalted butter
Lemon juice
Salt and pepper
100ml (approx) vegetable stock
30ml olive oil

Method:
1. Prepare the asparagus by snapping off the woody part of the stem, and then peel up to the spear (keeping the peelings). Blanch in a large pan of fast-boiling, heavily salted water. Refresh in iced water.
2. Next, use the asparagus peelings to make a coulis. Blanch in boiling salted water and then purée with a little vegetable stock, salt and olive oil to make a thin cream consistency.
3. Poach the eggs (see Top tip).
4. To make the hollandaise, clarify the butter by melting it in a small saucepan and warming it gently until there is a white foam on top. Skim off the foam, remove from the heat and allow to settle for 5 minutes. Pour the clear oil off, gently leaving the milk solids in the pan.
5. Whisk the egg yolk with 1 dessert spoon of hot water over a pan of simmering water. It will start to foam and then to thicken and become less bubbly. Remove from the water bath and gradually whisk in the hot clarified butter. The consistency should be similar to mayonnaise.
6. Season with the lemon juice, salt and pepper. The sauce should taste a little sharp to balance its richness.
7. To assemble, toast the muffins, warm the asparagus in a shallow pan with a knob of butter, seasoning and a little water. Fold a slice of ham onto each muffin half, lay on the warm asparagus spears and top with a soft-poached egg. Pour a generous spoonful of hollandaise sauce over the top and place briefly under a hot grill to glaze.

Sanjay Dwivedi

Sanjay Dwivedi offers a menu that encompasses his passion for his native India, his memories as a child and his almost military style French training in London. He is a cosmopolitan chef who has a light and subtle approach to his cuisine. At his restaurant Zaika he offers a delightful selection of uniquely creative dishes based on Indian classics.

Coconut Prawns with Steamed Rice

Chef Says

This dish means so much to me as it was the first dish I learnt to cook with my mother and I always remember making it with her in the kitchen at home.

Top tip - the prawns can be substituted with chicken breast or fish such as salmon, cod, scallops or halibut. The sauce can be made 3 days in advance.

Zaika
No.1 Kensington High Street
London W8 5NP
Telephone: 020 7795 6533
www.zaika-restaurant.co.uk

Serves: 4
Preparation time: 10 minutes
Cooking time: 10 minutes

Ingredients:

24 black tiger prawns, peeled and headless
1 teaspoon mustard seeds
2 fresh green chillies, chopped
1cm ginger, chopped
8 curry leaves (available from Indian supermarkets)
4 shallots, chopped
2 teaspoons turmeric
1 teaspoon ground coriander
1 teaspoon ground cumin
1 tin coconut milk
Olive oil

Method:

1. To a hot pan add 4 tablespoons of olive oil then splatter the mustard seeds in the pan until they start to jump (cook).
2. Add the green chillies, garlic and ginger and cook for 1 minute.
3. Now add the curry leaves and sauté for another minute.
4. Add the chopped shallots and cook for a further minute, follow this by adding the ground spices.
5. Continuously stir and add 4 tablespoons of water.
6. Now add the coconut milk and simmer for 5-10 minutes.
7. Taste for seasoning.
8. Add the prawns to the sauce and cook briefly for approximately 2 minutes until the prawns are cooked.
9. Serve with steamed rice.

ZAIKA

144
Stefano Stecca

The Brunello restaurant offers eclectic, modern Italian cuisine and was finalist for 'The Top Ten New Restaurants' category in the Evening Standard.

Grilled Duck Breast Marinated with Soy Sauce, Balsamic Vinegar, Sesame Oil, Grilled Aubergine and Avocado

Chef Says

I love this recipe as it fuses together mouth-watering Asian, Italian and French flavours. It is also a multi-seasonal dish which is delicious served both hot or warm.

Brunello Restaurant
Baglioni Hotel
Hyde Park Gate
Kensington
London SW7 5BB
Telephone: 020 7368 5700
www.baglionihotels.com

Serves: 1
Preparation time: **2 hours** including marinating
Cooking time: **10 minutes**

Ingredients:
1 duck breast
1 aubergine, grilled
4 slices of avocado

Sesame Marinade
30g rice vinegar
30g olive oil
90g soy sauce
15g balsamic vinegar
200g sesame oil
15g vinegar
Rock salt

Method:
1. Season the duck in rock salt and marinate in rice vinegar, olive oil, soy sauce, balsamic vinegar, sesame oil and vinegar for 2 hours.
2. Place the skin side of the duck on the grill and cook for 6 minutes and 2 minutes on the skinless side. Once the duck is pink, marinate for 5 minutes. Purée the aubergines and place on the plate.
3. To serve, thinly slice the duck and assemble with the sliced avocado on top of the purée of aubergines. Drizzle over the duck marinade and add the frisée salad as a finishing touch.

Steven Black

Steven Black worked in the kitchens of several Michelin starred country houses in the UK and Europe before coming to London. He came to the attention of London food critics first at 179 Shaftesbury Avenue. He moved to The Berkeley Square restaurant as Chef Patron in April 2003 where he has had critical acclaim for his light style of food at this elegant restaurant.

Roasted Scallops with Parsnip Purée and Seared Foie Gras

Chef Says

This dish is a signature dish of mine, which was created in 1999. It started as an idea of putting sweet scallops and smooth foie gras together to give an earthy taste of the foie gras and cèpes, and fresh taste of the scallop. These ingredients work extremely well together, and it has never been off my menu since, although I change the purée and mushrooms according to season.

Top tip - only use diver-caught scallops, as dredged scallops are bad for the seabed.

The Berkeley Square
7 Davies Street
London W1K 3DD
Telephone: 020 7629 6993
www.theberkeleysquare.com

Serves: **1**
Preparation time: **30 minutes**
Cooking time: **6 minutes**

Ingredients:

2 scallops
2 teaspoons tomato concasse
2 tablespoons parsnip purée
1 stick of salsify, peeled and sliced
1 slice of foie gras
Vegetable nage
Olive oil
2 large cèpes, sliced
25g butter
Lemon
Chervil

Method:

1. Heat a non-stick pan until very hot and then add a dash of olive oil. Season the scallops and add to the pan.
2. Pan-fry the cèpes and salsify, deglaze with the vegetable nage and a knob of butter.
3. Heat the parsnip purée (boil 1 parsnip in milk and liquidise).
4. Add the foie gras to a red-hot pan.
5. Turn over the scallops and add the lemon juice. Do not cook large scallops for more than 2½ minutes.
6. Plate the scallop dish; put 2 scallops on top of 2 small piles of tomato concassé. Put the purée diagonally going from 1 corner of the plate to the other (through the middle of the plate) in line with the scallops. Put the salsify and cèpe ragout on the opposite side of the scallops, place the foie gras and salsify stick on top. Garnish with a piece of chervil to finish.

Sue Manson and Maryann Wright

Y Polyn is run by Simon and Maryann Wright and Mark and Sue Manson. Between them they have earned an Egon Ronay Star and 2 AA Rosettes. In 2005 The Times named Y Polyn in the 'Top Ten places in the UK for Sunday Lunch' and later included the restaurant in their list of 'Top Ten New Restaurants' for 2005. Simon also works as a consultant on 'Gordon Ramsay's Kitchen Nightmares' and his own book 'Tough Cookies; Tales of Obsession, Toil and Tenacity from Britain's Kitchen Heavyweights' has just been published.

Rump of Salt Marsh Lamb with Garlic, Onion and Thyme Purée

Chef Says

As usual the key to success is in the shopping. We use Gower Salt Marsh lamb in season and find its flavour incomparable. The purée also works brilliantly with good pork chops and will keep for several days if covered and refrigerated.

Sue Manson and Maryann Wright
Y Polyn
Capel Dewi
Carmarthen SA32 7LH
Telephone: 01267 290000
www.ypolyn.com

Serves: 4
Preparation time: 1½ hours
Cooking time: 25 minutes

Ingredients:
4 rumps Salt Marsh lamb (approx 200g)
2 tablespoons olive oil
125g salted butter
4 large onions, peeled and thickly (2cm) diced
6 shallots, peeled and quartered
6 fat cloves of garlic, peeled and halved
6 sprigs of thyme
Maldon salt
Freshly ground black pepper

Method:
Garlic, Thyme and Onion Purée
1. Melt the butter in a thick-bottomed saucepan over a low heat and add the onions, shallots, garlic and the leaves from the thyme, a good pinch of salt and a grind of pepper.
2. Cook slowly for about an hour and a half until the mixture is soft and caramelised, stirring occasionally. Purée the mixture either in a processor or using a stick blender, put to one side and reheat when required.

Rump of Lamb
1. Season the lamb with salt and pepper. Heat the olive oil in the pan and when very hot put in the lamb, skin-side down. Sear each side until golden and put skin-side down into a pre-heated oven at 180ºC. Cook for approximately 15 minutes (pink).
2. Remove the lamb from the pan, cover and (importantly) rest for 5 minutes.
3. Slice the lamb into approximately 6 pieces and serve with the purée. Good with dauphinoise potatoes and some roasted Mediterranean vegetables.

150
Terry Miller

Terry, from Newcastle, found himself auditioning for 'Hell's Kitchen' without knowing it - his wife and son put him forward without telling him! He went on to win the show and has now opened his own restaurant, Rockafellas.

Rockafella

Chef Says

This recipe was the one that I made on the TV Series 'Hell's Kitchen'. People all over Britain, wherever I go mention my Rockafella and say they can't wait to try it.

Rockafellas
1 Amen Corner
The Side
Newcastle-upon-Tyne NE1 1PE
Telephone: 0191 242 3273

Serves: 1
Preparation time: 1 hour
Cooking time: 8 minutes

Ingredients:

Piping bag of mashed potato seasoned with white pepper and salt, cream and a little nutmeg
170g spinach
6 king prawns, shelled and cleaned
1 shallot, finely diced
½ litre fish stock
Knob of butter
1 small garlic clove
5ml English mustard
15ml parmesan, grated
Tabasco sauce
Fresh tarragon
1 fresh lemon
100ml double cream
50g cheddar cheese, grated

Method:

1. Boil the potatoes in salted water then drain. Make into mash potato by adding cream, butter and seasoning.
2. Put the spinach in boiling water for 10 seconds then cool in ice water.
3. Place the mash potato in a piping bag and pipe around the plate.
4. Place the spinach into 6 separate mounds on the plate.
5. Peel and clean the king prawns.
6. In a separate pan put a knob of butter and the garlic. Add the king prawns to seal them and then place onto the spinach mounds.
7. Add a drop of tabasco sauce to each king prawn.
8. In a separate pan add a knob of butter and the finely diced shallots, cook until soft. Then add the mustard, fish stock, double cream, finely grated parmesan and fresh chopped tarragon.
9. Cover the prawns with this sauce and top with grated cheese. Place in the oven at 200°C.

152
Tony Leck

Tony is a keen supporter of culinary competitions having both competed and judged nationally and internationally. He's no stranger to winning them either with 'Guernsey Restaurant of the Year' and 'Guernsey Ambassador of the Year 2000' to his name. His Ambassadorship was gained for leading the Guernsey Chefs Team to victory in the Craft Guild of Chefs '5 Nations Competition' promoting the Island's fresh quality produce.

Seared Scallops and Black Pudding with Creamed Celeriac and 'Pea Soup' Sauce

Chef Says

I first ate a similar dish many years ago in a Michelin rated restaurant in northern France, a superb dinner which avoided both the use of cream and potatoes! Somehow it relates to me as a Northerner now living in the Channel Isles. Similar to the famous lamb dish; 'Rack 'n' Black,' the scallops are sweet and superb with black pudding, and the potatoes are replaced with celeriac; a clean tasting dish full of down-to-earth good flavours.

Top tip - use a good supermarket or quality fishmonger to provide quality scallops. A good fishmonger will remove the scallops from their shell and also remove the skirt and any roe.

The Pavilion
Le Gron
St Saviour
Guernsey
Channel Islands
Telephone: 01481 264165

Serves: 2 for a main course or 4 as a starter
Preparation time: 30 minutes
Cooking time: 5 minutes
if all preparation is done

Ingredients:

12 scallops
150g horseshoe black pudding
1 small or medium celeriac
125g bag frozen peas, defrosted
50g onion, chopped
20g unsalted butter
2 rashers bacon
1 lemon
Salt, pepper and olive oil

Method:

1. Peel, wash and cut the celeriac into even-sized pieces, add to boiling salted water seasoned with a halved lemon.
2. When cooked, cool, refresh and drain the celeriac, liquidize (using some of the cooking liquor to thin down if required) and pass through a fine sieve setting aside.
3. Reheat when required either in a microwave or over a moderate heat in a saucepan, stirring continuously.
4. Slowly grill the bacon and cut into the desired shape, retain hot or reheat when ready to use.
5. Sauté the finely chopped onion in a little butter until translucent, add most of the bag of peas, cover with water from a boiling kettle and boil for a minute. Liquidize and pass through a fine sieve. Season with salt and pepper. Set the green sauce aside and add the remaining peas when ready to serve.

6. Slice the horseshoe black pudding into twelve even-sized discs, grill or sauté gently until evenly cooked and keep warm.
7. Brush each scallop with a little olive oil and sprinkle with a little sea salt. Place into a hot non-stick pan and cook for 30–45 seconds before turning the scallops over. Cook for a further 45–60 seconds before dishing up.
8. Remember, if too many scallops are placed into one pan this will reduce the required heat, so use two or more pans when cooking for larger numbers.

To Serve:

1. Place the scallops on top of the black pudding discs. Scoop or spoon the celeriac purée onto warm plates, add the scallops and black pudding, spoon the 'pea soup' sauce around the plate and add a crispy piece of bacon before serving.

Warren Lee

Warren started his career at Rules Restaurant in Covent Garden and then moved onto The Collection where he has been Head Chef for the past 8 years. Warren enjoys the freedom of not restricting himself to any particular theme, using a wide range of ingredients from Asian to European to create a menu that is always evolving.

Seared Foie Gras with Seaweed Sauce and Crispy Won Tons

Chef Says

When cooking foie gras, use a non-stick pan and season the liver with salt and pepper before you pan-fry.

The Collection Restaurant
264 Brompton Road
London SW3 2AS
Telephone: 020 7225 1212
www.the-collection.co.uk

Serves: 4
Preparation time: 30 minutes
Cooking time: 10 minutes

Ingredients:
4 x 100g slices of foie gras, deveined
8 sheets of won ton skins
3 spring onions
5g wakame seaweed
15ml soy sauce
15ml sushi vinegar
1 litre chicken stock
Salt and pepper

Method:
Sauce
1. Pour a little hot water over the seaweed and leave for 10 minutes to soften. Refresh in cold water then drain and chop finely.
2. Reduce the chicken stock to a quarter of its original size then mix together with the sushi vinegar, soy sauce and the seaweed. Keep warm.

Won Ton
1. Fry the won ton skins at 180°C, 350°F until they become crispy and golden brown. Drain on kitchen paper and leave aside. This should take 2-3 minutes.

Spring Onions
1. Wash and peel the outer layer then slice very thinly at an angle.

To Serve:
1. Heat up the pan and seal the foie gras on both sides for approximately 3-4 minutes. Place in a hot oven at 190°C, 375°F for a further 5-7 minutes.
2. Place one won ton on a plate, fill with some spring onions then place the foie gras on top. Spoon some of the sauce over and around, then finally add the other won ton, slightly off centre.

Saltimbocca - This is an Italian dish of sautéed veal scallops and prosciutto which is braised in white wine.

Prosciutto - An aged, dry-cured spiced Italian ham that is usually sliced thinly and served without cooking.

Wasabi - A very pungent green Japanese condiment made from the root of the herb Eutrema Wasabi.

Bain-Marie - A large pan containing hot water in which smaller pans are placed to cook food slowly or to keep food warm.

Refresh - Once vegetables are tender when boiling, plunge into ice cold water to stop them over-cooking. They can be warmed through when ready to serve.

Carpaccio - Very thinly sliced raw meat or fish, garnished with a sauce.

Chinois - A conical mesh sieve for straining sauces and soups.

Monte - When melting a solid like butter, gently lap the liquid around the saucepan. This gives a continuous heat which speeds up the melting process.

Barley Miso - Miso is a fermented soybean paste, essential in Japanese cooking. It has the consistency of creamy peanut butter and will keep indefinitely if refrigerated in a closed container.

Al dente - Cooked enough to be firm but not soft.

Clarify - To make liquids such as coffee or soups completely transparent by adding egg white. After several minutes heating the egg white in the liquid, the white coagulates, collecting solids in it. This can then be strained off, leaving a completely clear liquid.

Salsify - This is a European plant which has grass like leaves and purple flower heads. The root of the plant is eaten as a vegetable.

Okra - A tall tropical Asian annual plant widely cultivated in warm regions. The edible pods are used in soups and as a vegetable.

Cèpes - A large edible mushroom found in woodlands. They have a thick rounded brown cap. Also called porcino.

Deglaze - After foods are cooked in a pan on the stove or in the oven, the pan is deglazed. This means liquid is added to loosen and dissolve the brown bits and drippings that form at the bottom of the pan during cooking and basting. This gives you all the flavour from the cooked food. Deglazing liquid is usually broth, a marinade, or wine, and is the first step to cooking many sauces.

Julienne - Cut into long thin strips.

Kohl Rabi - Part of the mustard family. The base of the Kohl Rabi stem is eaten as a vegetable. It is also known as a turnip cabbage.

Conversion Guide

Temperature

Gas	Electric	Electric
	Degrees F	Degrees C
1	275	140 very low
2	300	150 very low
3	325	170 low
4	350	180 moderate
5	375	190 fairly hot
6	400	200 hot
7	425	220 hot
8	455	230 very hot

Weights

1oz	25g
2	50g
3	75g
4	110g
5	150g
6	175g
7	200g
8	225g
9	250g
10	275g
12	350g
1lb	450g
1.5lb	700g
2lb	900g
3lb	1.3kg

Liquids

2fl oz	60ml
3	90ml
5	150ml
10	300ml
15	450ml
1 pint	600ml
1.25	750ml
1.75	1 litre
2	1.2 litres
2.5	1.5 litres

131

90

Travel in style – Win a journey on board the Orient-Express in the UK.

There is something very romantic about riding by train through the countryside in the most sumptuous surroundings, whilst being served the finest of food and your every need looked after by an attentive steward. Relax amidst the luxurious splendour of the elegant carriages of Northern Belle, crafted on the classic 'Belle' trains of the 1930's or the vintage art deco interiors of its sister train British Pullman carriages of the Orient-Express, whilst enjoying a cultural day out or unforgettable dining experience.

Sip a glass of chilled champagne en-route to Cambridge, Brighton or Bath on British Pullman, or York, Wimbledon or Kew Gardens on Northern Belle; just some of the 500 days out and luxurious weekend breaks on offer from Orient-Express throughout the year. Typically your Orient-Express journey begins with a mid-morning departure, after which brunch is served with bucks fizz. When you arrive at your chosen destination enjoy a tour or free time before rejoining the train for dinner with champagne and wine during the homeward journey.

Orient-Express is offering one lucky reader the chance to win a day trip for 2 people up to the total value of £600 on either its British Pullman or Northern Belle trains in the UK.

All you have to do is answer this question:
The Executive Head Chef of Orient-Express UK is featured in 'This is my Favourite' - What is his name?

To enter, simply go online to www.thisismyfavourite.co.uk or send a postcard with your answer to Orient-Express Competition, This is my Favourite, Westwood Centre, Nutwood Way, Southampton SO40 3SZ. Closing date 31st December 2006.

The prize is valid for 12 months from the day the winner is informed and is subject to availability. There is no cash alternative. The British Pullman departs from London Victoria and the Northern Belle from various regional cities including Manchester, Leeds, Birmingham and Newcastle. For an Orient-Express 'Journeys in the UK' brochure or further information on all Orient-Express departures call 0845 077 2222 or visit www.orient-express.com.

We knew from printing last year's book how important it would be to choose the right paper for our second edition. Food images and portraits, all from different sources, yet all needing to look their best. Quite a challenge for any paper!

Also, this time we wanted to use a recycled stock. Given the charitable ethos underlying the book supporting BBC Children in Need, it is appropriate that we should do our best to both respect the environment and show our commitment to sound environmental practice.

Greencoat Matt and Greencoat Plus Velvet proved the ideal solution - high bulk to give the book the right 'feel', plus sharpness and definition to those all-important images; the right creative look, the right environmental credentials, with 80% post-consumer recycled content, and available in a wide range of weights and sizes.

Cover printed on Greencoat Plus Velvet 300g/m^2 and text pages printed on Greencoat Matt 130g/m^2, supplied by Howard Smith Paper and manufactured by Marchi, Italy.

Simon Marshall, The Ransom Group.

Published by The Ransom Group

© The Ransom Group 2006

BBC Children in Need Appeal Commercial Participation Number CMC/05/10

Printed in Great Britain by Butler and Tanner Ltd.

ISBN 0-9551331-1-4

This is my Favourite
Westwood Centre
Nutwood Way
Southampton SO40 3SZ
info@thisismyfavourite.co.uk
www.thisismyfavourite.co.uk

BBC Children in Need Appeal is a registered charity, no.802052